BRAND ADVERTISING

How to Create Work that Connects with Customers Every Time

Stephen Hawley Martin

Stephen Hawley Martin, Senior Partner of Hawley Martin Parters, is a former principal and Senior Vice President of The Martin Agency who has developed Brand Advertising and communications plans for dozens of clients. Among them are BB&T, Virginia Tourism, Colonial Williamsburg, Mobil Oil, Eskimo Pie, Alcoa, two divisions of General Motors, a number of Nestlé Company brands, and Dominion Virginia Power. He is the only three-time winner of the *Writer's Digest* Book Award, which he won for the metaphysical thriller, *The Mt. Pelée Redemption,* the whodunit, *Death in Advertising,* and a nonfiction book about an ancestor hanged as a witch in 1692 Salem, Massachusetts, *A Witch in the Family. The Mt. Pelée Redemption* also won *Independent Press* magazine's first prize for visionary fiction. *Lean Transformation,* a business management title he ghostwrote, has been translated into half a dozen languages, and one he edited about the Toyota product development system, *Product Development for the Lean Enterprise,* has changed the way many major companies develop new products. Contact him at Stephen@HawleyMartin.com

Bruce Goldman

Bruce Goldman's advertising career has taken him to some of the world's best agencies, including Young & Rubicam and DDB in New York; Beber Silverstein & Partners and HDC in Florida; and DDB Needham in Melbourne, Australia. As Hawley Martin LLC's Strategic Partner for Creative, he has worked with Steve Martin to develop and apply the Lean Agency and Brand Advertising concepts. His work has won more than 400 regional, national and international awards, including Clio statuettes, One Show Gold and Silver Pencils, Silver and Bronze New York Festivals Worldmedals, and Silver and Bronze Effie awards for advertising effectiveness. Bruce has judged international advertising competitions, taught advertising writing at the School of Visual Arts in New York and Virginia Commonwealth University School of Mass Communications. He wrote Your Check Is in the Mail, a national non-fiction best-seller on consumer credit, and almost 500 columns on advertising for Examiner.com. In addition to being a strategic partner of Hawley Martin, Bruce heads his own creative boutique, Bright Orange Advertising. To get in touch with Bruce, send him an email at BGoldman@BrightOrangeAdv.com.

BRAND ADVERTISING

How to Create Work that Connects with Customers Every Time

by

Stephen Hawley Martin

and

Bruce Goldman

RICHMOND, VIRGINIA

Brand Advertising: How to Create Work that Connects with Customers Every Time © 2003, 2008, 2013 & 2016 by Stephen Hawley Martin and Bruce Goldman. All rights reserved. No part of this book may be used or reproduced in any manner whatsoever without written permission except in the case of brief quotations embodied in critical articles and reviews.

Contents

Preface
Why People in Charge of Marketing
Need to Know about Brand Advertising — Page 7

Chapter One:
Minds vs. Hearts — Page 15

Chapter Two:
Numbers vs. Reality — Page 24

Chapter Three:
Don't let it be forgot
That once there was a spot
For one brief, shining moment
That was known as Camelot. — Page 15

Chapter Four:
Many hands vs. too many cooks — Page 50

Chapter Five:
Leading sacred cows to slaughter. — Page 72

Chapter Six:
The shortest distance between Point A and Point B
isn't necessarily the fastest way to get there. — Page 86

Chapter Seven:
Why Fat Agencies stay that way. — Page 113

"I know half my advertising budget is wasted.
I just don't know which half.

– John Wanamaker (1838 – 1922)

Preface

Why People in Charge of Marketing Need to Know about Brand Advertising

It should go without saying that the changes that have taken place in advertising and marketing communications over the past 30 years have been nothing less than astounding. When I first started in the advertising agency business, there wasn't much that could be done for a client if the client did not have at least a few million dollars to spend. About the only way to attract the eyeballs of potential customers back then was to purchase what has now come to be known as traditional media—radio, television, magazines, newspaper ads, or billboards.

Nowadays, with some artful search engine optimization,[1] or a cool video that goes viral, many thousands, perhaps even many millions of customers' eyeballs can be had for as little as a few hundred bucks. That's good because it gives a fighting chance to those trying to get a business off the ground on a shoestring.

One result, however, is that the leaders of small budget businesses typically work with people who know a fair amount about the Internet, websites and apps, but very little, if anything at all, about branding and connecting on an emotional level with potential customers. While these folks may generate millions of views on YouTube and good rankings on Google searches, the communications they create may or may not actually lead to sales, or to the amount of sales they could.

To be effective, marketing communications have to do more than simply get attention. They have to create a bond between the customer and the product. They have to create, as my brother David used to say, "An expectation of performance," a phrase he used often to sum up his definition of a brand.

This book will condense what my colleague, Bruce Goldman, and I have learned over the last 30+ years about creating what I call "Brand Advertising." The term applies in this book to all forms of marketing communications, from websites and webinars to viral videos. If it helps build a bond with prospective customers, a bond that creates an expectation of performance, it's Brand Advertising.

Let me set the stage with a little history. When my brother David and I sold our interest in The Martin Agency, we started a new ad firm we named after our dad called Hawley Martin Partners. We did it to honor him. You see, he'd been ad man, too. His biggest claim to fame was the brand icon he created for Land O'Lakes, the

American Indian that still graces the packaging of that product line today.

Hawley was a New York native who studied at the University of Arizona, and his first job after college was as the foreman of a ranch near Tucson. We thought it was interesting and ironic that he had started out branding cattle and had ended up branding products.

The new agency took off like a rocket. After only a couple of years, it was bought by the advertising agency holding company, Interpublic. Three years after that, it was purchased by Arnold Worldwide.

During the time following the Interpublic purchase, I realized there were aspects of being a minnow in the ocean of a big organization I didn't like. So I took the opportunity when it presented itself and exited Hawley Martin before Arnold took over as the new ocean.

I set up my office in the pool house on my brother's property and started making my living writing books as well as working directly with companies—creating marketing communications for them and helping them turn products into brands. Bruce Goldman was one of the advertising pros I partnered with back then, and we still work together, today.

I also ghostwrote some books, and I edited some others. One I ghostwrote called *Lean Transformation: How to Change Your Business into a Lean Enterprise* became an international business best seller. Another I edited that sold very well was called *Product Development for the Lean Enterprise: Why Toyota's System is Four Times More Productive and How You Can Implement It*. These books have been translated into other languages, including: Chinese, Korean, Russian, Spanish, Italian, and German.

I learned a great deal from writing and editing those books. It was not long before it occurred to me the techniques they taught could be applied to the marketing communications side of my business. As a result, Bruce and I began putting this newly-acquired knowledge to work when creating Brand Advertising to connect and build bonds between our clients and their potential customers.

By now just about everyone who hasn't been living in a cave knows that the manufacturing sector has just about universally gone Lean. Why? Because Toyota has shown the world that lean manufacturing — which essentially means eliminating waste and keeping things moving — produces higher quality products at the lowest possible prices.

But what does this have to do with advertising?

A lot. When an entire company goes Lean, it's not just manufacturing that's affected. A Lean Enterprise is one that's run by empowered teams—the clumsy and ineffective bureaucracy having been eliminated. And being a Lean Enterprise doesn't stop at making the people closest to a problem the ones to solve it. Toyota's *product development* system, for example, has as much to do with the success of that company as the Toyota Production System. Aside from creating great cars, the company's development system is also virtually waste free. This is so because it is a very different approach to developing products than that used in the West. According to the National Center for Manufacturing Sciences, as well as studies by others, Toyota's development engineers are four times as productive as their U.S. counterparts.

How so? In the West, engineers focus on developing new vehicles in a linear fashion, the same way most ad agencies develop ad campaigns. At Toyota, engineers focus on learning as much as possible and using that knowledge to develop great vehicles without false starts, or in the jargon used by engineers, loopbacks.

In contrast, Western engineers define several product concepts and select the one that has the most promise — the same as creative personnel in an ad agency do with ads. Engineers draw up specifications and partition them into subsystems. The subsystems are designed, built, and rolled up for system testing. When results aren't up to snuff, as is often the case, the team reworks the specs and the designs accordingly — an inherently unproductive and confusing endeavor. The same thing happens with ad concepts that are selected early on, polished to perfection, and then shown to clients or consumer panels only to be shot down. But this doesn't have to be.

Another way to think of Toyota's system is "test and design" rather than the traditional "design and test." The idea is to learn first what is going to work and then design around that. This is why some have dubbed the Toyota system the Learn First Product Development System.

In the 1997 model year, Toyota introduced a new Camry. Ford introduced a new Taurus to compete with it. With the 1997 Camry priced just $600 more than its predecessor and the '97 Taurus almost $1,000 more than the '96 model, Toyota had a $1,300—or almost 8 percent—price advantage. The next model year, 1998, Lean Enterprise lowered the Camry's cost by $350, while business as usual raised the Taurus's by $385. This increased the Camry's edge to $2,035, or slightly more than 12 percent. Moreover, Toyota achieved this edge not by sacrificing quality, but by increasing it, as evidenced by its glowing *Consumer Reports* and car magazine reviews.

The Lean Enterprise revolution is by no means confined to manufacturers. In the December 7, 2002, *Wall Street Journal*, Rainer Meckes and

Brand Advertising

Felix Krohn chronicled how ignoring its principles brought Reuters to "the deepest financial crisis of its 150-year history. Its market capitalization has plunged by almost 90 percent from its peak. And last month it lost a billion-dollar contract with Merrill Lynch to Thomson Financial. It's not only losing money for the first time ever. It may also lose its place in the FTSE 100 index." In February, 2003, Reuters announced a $631 million loss and 3,000 job cuts.

From its start in 1851, Reuters had built its financial- and general-news business on the latest communications technology—the telegraph, the Transatlantic cable, the teleprinter, the computer. But somewhere around the 1980s it seemed to start relying on another form of technology—the autopilot.

While Reuters kept doing the same old same old, a former Wall Street stock analyst named Michael Bloomberg had the idea of adding financial analysis tools to real-time pricing and other data like those that Reuters provided. This plus instant messaging, another new technology Reuters ignored, ate part of their lunch. Meanwhile, Thomson Financial, another new upstart, figured out how to offer the same bare-bones financial information that Reuters did, but at deep discounts. And there went the part of 90 percent of Reuters' business that Bloomberg didn't swallow.

If the Lean Enterprise revolution isn't afoot in your company, maybe it's at work for your competitors. You know, the ones who undercut your lowest possible, distress-sale pricing, but still beat your profit margin. Who fill orders the same day they come in, but with a fraction of your production and warehousing capacity. Or who have infinitesimal defect rates without a single full-time quality inspector.

And if there's no sign of Lean Enterprise in either your company or its competitors, just look around. Know why your computer probably runs on Intel, rather than National Semiconductor or Fairchild microchips? Why Southwest Airlines continues to fly high while United Airlines and U. S. Airways had to go bankrupt before getting it together, and American Airlines remains in bankruptcy? Why UPS commercials sell not on-time delivery, but inventory control?

Lean Enterprise, that's why.

Of course, if all this has escaped your day-to-day business attention, you have at least a partial excuse. Because of all the aspects of your company's business, marketing has been among the last to join the Lean Enterprise revolution. Most advertising agencies make it difficult to impossible for their clients, the marketing departments like yours, to do so. Because once you peel away their high-tech veneer, most agencies still run according to principles which took form in the mid-1960s. Before cable television. Before shopping malls, big-box and category-killer stores. Before the resurgence of catalog sales. Before telemarketing and spam. Before Asian competition and the graying of America. Before Amazon.com and discount travel websites.

Your company doesn't turn out its products the same way it did in the Sixties, so you wouldn't think ad agencies do. After all, haven't they gone from ten employees per million dollars' billings to less than one over the past four decades? Computers have eliminated a bunch of agency jobs, like copy typist, type director and paste-up artist. But that shrinkage of the staff-to-billings ratio is more a matter of inflation than leanness. It's a testimony to the fact that $1 million buys far less newspaper or magazine space, less television or radio time, than it used to. Less actual advertising for the money means fewer people needed to produce it.

Yes, your agency has computers out the wazoo. Yes, it's got sophisticated-sounding consumer research tools. Yes, they use nonlinear video editing and morphs and CGI. But get past all that, and there's a basic structure that's still wearing love beads, granny glasses and bell bottoms.

That's why it takes so many talented people to spend so much time and money accomplishing so relatively little. Why companies like yours can waste months of time and tens of thousands of dollars on well thought out, intelligently justified, brilliantly designed and written, beautifully presented campaigns that are . . . well, wrong.

It's all in the structure.

The genius of Lean Enterprise is that it creates a new structure that institutionalizes efficiency instead of waste. That makes high quality and low cost symbiotic instead of antithetic. That tears down walls between specialists rather than erecting them. That makes everyone, especially the customer (which, for your advertising agency, is you) the focus of the whole process.

We first learned of Lean Enterprise in 1995, when a client of ours who manufactured appliance controls switched over to it and wanted to base manufactured appliance controls switched over to it and wanted to base his advertising strategy on using the advantages of Lean Production as brand and product differentiators in a commodity category. In order to do the campaign, we had to learn about the process. And the more we learned, the more impressed with it we became. Why, we asked ourselves, couldn't the same kind of streamlining, the same kind of waste elimination, continuous flow, uncompartmentalized thinking and constant improvement also work for advertising agencies? It can, and very well—at least as we've applied it to our own agency.

In the following chapters, you'll learn more about this structure, and how it could and should work in the agencies you rely on for your marketing and advertising ideas and materials. This structure is the marketing equivalent of Lean Enterprise, so we call it Lean Marketing or, for advertising agencies, Lean Advertising. In the near-term future, it will revolutionize your operations—just as it's already revolutionized other parts of your company's business. So the choice is really very simple. You can bring Lean Marketing to the ways your brand is advertised and marketed. Or, like Reuters, you can sit back, relax, and wait for the competition to bring the revolution to you.

Stephen Hawley Martin

Brand Advertising

These ads show how Lean Production revolutionized manufacturing. Applying its principles can revolutionize your advertising.

Brand Advertising

Chapter One
Minds vs. Hearts

If you've ever taken Marketing 101 or the equivalent, you've learned about the different types of purchase decisions. There are high-commitment and low-commitment purchases and considered (i.e., highly rational) and impulse (i.e., highly emotional) decisions.

The working assumption is that impulse decisions usually correlate with low-commitment purchases and considered decisions with high-commitment purchases.

After all, it's only rational, right?

The problem is, human beings aren't.

That's why a teenage girl will spend hours, maybe days (considered decision), agonizing over which shade of lipstick or eye shadow to buy (low-commitment purchase).

Or why the old real-estate agent trick of having cookies baking in the oven when showing a house to prospective buyers works more often than not to make the sale. Since buying a house is the biggest financial decision most people make in their lifetimes, it should be a highly rational, deeply considered one. Yet the emotional stimulus of that baking-cookie aroma overrides rationality.

That's because, except for Mr. Spock (who, any Trekkie will tell you, was only half human) nobody makes decisions rationally.

Facts about your brand are important to your audience, but only secondarily. People make purchase decisions–even business purchase decisions–on the basis of emotion, then marshal facts and rational arguments to justify their emotional decision.

If you don't believe us, just ask University of Virginia psychology professor Jonathan Haidt, or read his 2012 book, *The Righteous Mind: Why Good People are Divided by Politics and Religion.*

After a massive online survey, in which researchers asked people moral questions, timed their responses and scanned their brains, Haidt found that people are fundamentally intuitive, not rational. The fact is, that if you want to persuade others, you have to appeal to their sentiments. We were never designed to listen to reason. When you ask people moral questions, time their responses and scan their brains, their answers and brain activation patterns indicate that they reach conclusions quickly and produce reasons later only to justify what they've decided.

The problem isn't that people don't reason. They do reason. But their arguments aim to support their conclusions, not yours. Reason doesn't work like a judge or teacher, impartially weighing evidence or guiding us to wisdom. It works more like a lawyer or press secretary, justifying our acts and judgments to others.

We compete for social status, and the key advantage in this struggle is the ability to influence others. Reason, in this view, evolved to help us spin, not to help us learn. So if you want to change people's minds, Haidt concludes, don't appeal to their reason. Appeal to reason's boss...[1]

And, as any competent ad person could have told the good professor, that boss is emotion.

For at least half a century, advertising practitioners have known that people make purchase decisions with their hearts, not their heads; that they make an emotional leap to a product or brand decision, then build a bridge of logic afterwards to support it.

This is why most of the new-car ad readers are people who just bought that make of car and are looking to justify their purchase—and why, back when Ogilvy & Mather handled the Mercedes advertising, they filled long-copy ads with facts and figures that would reassure a new owner, not lure a new prospect.

It's why consumers buy from brands whose personalities they like and shun others, often with better products, whose personalities they don't.

It's why, as we mentioned before, realtors tell homeowners to have cookies baking in the oven when they show the house to prospective buyers—and why there are four, count 'em, four products on Amazon's site which give cars that new-car smell.

And it's why even heartless monopolies like the Bell System were able to get people to make more (then-expensive) long-distance calls back in the '70s with tear-jerking television commercials and slogans like "Reach Out and Touch Someone."

If you doubt the power of hearts over heads, advertising for the 2012 summer Olympics provides a handy controlled experiment. While most campaigns gravitated to Olympic history, multicultural glorification of athletics or health messages (all rational), two went straight for the heartstrings.

Omega's campaign, for example, was about the fact that their clocks and watches have been timing 25 different Olympic games over 80 years. Over the Rolling Stones' "Start Me Up" as the audio track, they showed a montage of multinational, multicultural, multiethnic, minority and majority, male and female athletes psyching themselves up for the start of their respective events. The athletes included "Chinese diver Qiu Bo, U.S. swimmer Natalie Coughlin, British heptathlete Jessica Ennis, U.S. sprinter Tyson Gay, South African swimmer Chad Le Clos and U.S. pole vaulter Jenn Suhr," according to Omega's description of the commercial on YouTube.

Two major advertisers—Coke and McDonald's—seemed to be talking to a target audience of two—First Lady and anti-obesity crusader Michelle Obama and Michael Bloomberg, the New York mayor who banned transfats, salt and large sodas from public eating places citywide until the courts made him stop.

As makers of the number-one and number-two brands of soda (Coke and Diet Coke), Coca-Cola must have been feeling particularly defensive. Katie Bayne, president and general manager, sparkling beverages, Coca-Cola North America, claimed in an email to Ad Age, "We have a timeless commitment to enhance well-being in all of its forms. Encouraging people to get active, and providing them with opportunities to do so, has always been at the heart of our brand values."[2]

As evidence of this, she said, Coca-Cola was the first soda brand to voluntarily put calorie information on the front of nearly all of its bottles and cans, and of the 700 beverages the company produces, 150 (all of 21.4% of its product lineup) were now low-calorie and no-calorie.

Coke produced two campaigns—one for the U. S. and one for everywhere else—to motivate couch potatoes worldwide to get up and start working off the empty calories they consumed from chugging one of the 79% of the company's other brands.

Brand Advertising

The non-U.S. version resembled nothing so much as a Super Bowl halftime show. Over a song called "Move to the Beat" were clips of the usual assortment of multinational, multicultural, multiethnic, minority and majority, male and female athletes at their respective sports, intercut with shots of a conductor, British singer Katy B and dancers all moving in sync to the beat of this song.

Domestically, they showed an "8-pack" of athletes—hurdler David Oliver, gymnast Shawn Johnson, woman boxer Marlen Esparza, wrestler Henry Cejudo, tennis player John Isner, soccer player Alex Morgan, diver David Boudia and Paralympic swimmer Jessica Long -- chosen, according to Ad Age, "to represent a diversity of sports as well as the multicultural make-up of American youth."

Video showed them competing at their sports—and, incidentally, drinking full-sugar Coke in such places as the wrestling ring and the swimming pool—with audio saying that you can support them in their quest for speed, toughness, strength and happiness by buying specially marked cans of non-diet Coke.

McDonald's played "I am not a crook" on a multimedia level.

According to global brand officer Kevin Newell, who was a 200-meter Olympic trials runner in 1980, the "fundamental principal [sic]" behind their Olympics advertising campaign was to "encourage fun, active play as well as smart eating."[3]

The way they did this in one commercial was to show kids from different countries around the world racing each other to McDonald's for such healthy dishes as french fries and Happy Meals, followed by basketball players LeBron James and Luol Deng challenging each other to a one-on-one game, with a Big Mac and fries for the winner.

Online, they created a website, championsofplay.com, in 41 different languages and featuring athletes "who will inspire kids to get active," Newell claimed.

This physical activity consisted of playing virtual swimming across the Atlantic and going online to chat with Olympic athletes—neither of which could burn off so much as the calories in one McDonald's french fry, since the only exercise kids got was for their thumbs.

While Omega, Pepsi, McDonald's, Cadbury, Adidas and other advertisers ran rational commercials, two brands went emotional.

Brand Advertising

Over the long term, Nike advertising has featured professional and well-known amateur athletes and built their message around glorifying the fact that they, uh, just do it. But for the Olympics, Nike created an ambush, almost anti-Olympics, campaign that ran on non-Olympic television programming.

This campaign celebrated the democratization of athletics. Over and over again, the voice-over made the point that "greatness isn't reserved for the chosen few in one special city." The establishing commercial showed athletes of all ages and abilities in London, Ohio; London, Norway; London, Ontario; Little London, Jamaica; Small London, Nigeria; East London, South Africa, and other Londons throughout the world putting forth effort to find their greatness (which was the campaign's theme).

Individual commercials went on to slice and dice the message by sport. One showed an overweight jogger from London, Ohio. Another, a Little League baseball pitcher playing with no left hand. Others showed skateboarding, high diving, gymnastics, soccer, water polo and wheelchair racing. There was even a weightlifter straining in closeup as he does his reps while the voice-over says that sometimes the precious metal that greatness is measured in is iron.

When you watch the campaign (and you still can, on YouTube), your heart goes out to the one-handed Little Leaguer and to the 12-year-old fat kid jogging to lose weight. And, if you do any kind of exercise at all, you feel just great about yourself—and maybe Nike too.

Procter & Gamble produced a campaign that destroyed the reputation it had built over decades for producing commercials that are strategically smart but creatively dumb—for treating ad campaigns like scientific laboratory experiments, where the only variables allowed were ones they could control and adjust to see what effect each would have in the marketplace. Creativity, not being such a variable, was kept mediocre as a constant.

For each commercial they ended up running, they'd commission literally hundreds of storyboards on many different strategies. From this, they'd narrow down to a handful to submit to focus group testing, then cull further to produce two or three to run in test markets. They'd determine which parts of which commercials worked best, then play mix and match to end up building a final commercial the way Dr. Frankenstein built men.

The results were just what they wanted: consistent. Consistently safe, consistently middle-of-the-road, consistently predictable, consistently boring. And if they were consistently too dull to catch consumers' attention, well, as the world's largest advertiser, P&G could afford to keep running and running and running and running them until viewers had no escape.

But for the 2012 Olympics, P&G launched what global brand-building officer Marc Pritchard described as "the most far-reaching and ambitious campaign" in the package-goods giant's history[4]. It covered 34 brands, ran in 73 countries—and broke just about every advertising rule that P&G imposed on its agencies over the decades.

At a time when television screens were inundated with spots showing athletes doing their thing and glorifying their brands' roles in making that possible; when the air waves were filled with sanctimonious ads lecturing about such highfalutin' subjects as Diversity, Physical Activity and Health; when every advertiser was a "proud sponsor of the 2012 Olympics"; P&G's ad campaign did something completely different. It glorified and emotionally connected with its target audience.

There's this flawed theory about advertising that runs during televised sportscasts, and that's that the only thing viewers are capable of paying attention to is more footage of the sport being televised, because they're so dumb, they'll think it's part of the action, not a commercial. That's why you see all those spots with auto-racing footage during the Indy 500 telecast, football footage during NFL games...and Olympic sports footage during commercials that run before and during the Olympics.

But P&G's Olympics advertising wasn't really about the Olympics. It was about their audience—the mothers of the world who raise and take care of their kids with love and hard work (and buy Procter & Gamble products, but the spots don't talk about that). So while viewers saw some Olympic-type footage, it was with a twist, and only in a supporting role. The stars of the commercials were mothers.

Having chosen this strategy, Procter & Gamble went all the way with it.

They even eschewed the cliched "Proud sponsors of the Olympic games" signoff and instead used the campaign line, "Proud sponsors of Moms" to end all their television commercials and viral videos. That one line, by the way, was about half of the entire commercial or video's copy.

The rest was pure, visual storytelling and emotion.

One 60-second execution, for example, showed all the usual Olympic events, from the opening parade to the finish line, but with a difference: All the "athletes" in their national uniforms were children. As we saw a young boy on the high-diving board, the camera cut to a closeup of his mother looking up anxiously from the audience. Then, against a pure white screen, we saw a super: To their moms, they'll always be kids. The super was then replaced by quick cuts of five P&G brand logos while a female voice-over said, "P&G. Proud sponsors of moms."

But the real winner of the campaign was a commercial-and-video pair with the visual focus almost purely on mothers in one country after another, as they wake up their children before the crack of dawn, feed them breakfast, get them to school, take them to and support them during after-school sports training, tend to their sports injuries, and then, as their children have grown up, put their hearts and souls in to rooting for them at the Olympic games themselves. "The world's toughest job," says the end super of the two-minute video, "is the world's best job. Thank you, Mom." Then came the almost unobtrusive product logos and that line again: "P&G. Proud sponsor of Moms."

The 30-second commercial conveyed the same thought more succinctly: "Behind every athlete is a loving Mom. Thank you, Mom."

Unlike their usual mediocrities, Procter & Gamble didn't have to keep running these spots until people noticed them, because they're the kind of messages you want to see, and get a lump in your throat over, and enjoy, again and again—and that's something we never dreamed we'd be writing about a P&G commercial.

Here we have a clear-cut case of rational versus emotional advertising campaigns. They ran at the same time, on the same channel, with the same programming and reached the same audience. The only real variable was the nature of the messages themselves.

So how'd they do? For the most part, not so hot.

According to a representative sample of 1,034 respondents to a Toluna Global Omnibus online survey, only 7% could identify Cadbury as an Olympic sponsor, for example, and only 17% UPS and British Air.

To make matters worse, a substantial proportion of consumers thought some brands' Olympic advertising came from their main competitors. Half as many respondents (19%) incorrectly identified Burger King as a sponsor instead of correctly naming McDonald's (40%). While 47% thought Coke was a sponsor (correctly), 28% thought it was rival Pepsi. Even worse than that, more consumers thought that Olympic advertising from Adidas was from arch-competitor Nike (24% vs 37%), who didn't even advertise there.

Adding injury to insult, small majorities and a large plurality of consumers said the Olympic sponsorships made them feel more positive about the brands that weren't being advertised—48% for Pepsi, 52% for Burger King and 54% for Nike.

When MediaCom Sport monitored 25 Olympic advertisers' Twitter activity for not only number of tweets, but also for positivity or negativity, they came up with similar findings.

Of the 25 Olympic sponsors tracked, each of whom spent in the nine figures on two weeks' advertising, McDonald's finished dead last. This wasn't because consumers didn't notice or respond to their campaign, but because they really didn't like it.

According to MediaCom Sport's global head Marcus John, the campaign provoked hugely negative sentiment about the "perceived contradiction of the brand's Olympic association given general health concerns" about all the salty, sugary and fatty fast foods that are McDonald's stock in trade.

This contradiction between what McDonald's commercials said and what McDonald's serves was "the dominant trend in conversation," he told MediaPost News[5]. "[C]oupled with the extensive reach of the brand, [this] ensures the McDonald's score remains significantly negative."

The emotion-driven P&G campaign, in contrast, "attract[ed] very little negative sentiment" compared to McDonald's, John said, so while P&G had "comparatively less reach across Twitter" than McDonald's and other brands, more positive sentiment helped helped it go for, and win, the Olympic advertising gold.

One of the first and most important lessons a budding copywriter learns about writing effective advertising is that "if you have to call it something, it ain't."

When your main product is greaseburgers and fries, all the high-minded but empty factual-sounding lectures about health and physical activity in the world aren't going to cut it with your audience. Because from

Brand Advertising

Richmond, Virginia, to Richmond, England, they can spot hypocrisy a mile away (or, in the case of Richmond, England, 1.60934 kilometres away).

And when you glorify your audience by showing you truly understand what their lives are about, they can spot that, too—and show their appreciation in the marketplace.

It's great that P&G finally learned that lesson. And a great shame that McDonald's didn't.

Now, your brand may not have the deep pockets of the world's largest advertiser. But even without the original music score, without the cast of dozens and hundreds of extras, without all the international location shooting, you can still do what P&G did right:

1. Make your advertising about your audience, not your product. And talk to them, not at them. People care about themselves, not you; that's human nature.
2. Keep it clean and simple. Research shows that viewers can absorb 1.25 ideas from a 30-second commercial—and that's only if they're paying attention. (See point 5 below.)
3. Emotions trump laundry lists of product features. You're spending all this money to make your prospective customers feel good, not yourself. And people make purchase decisions emotionally, then use sales points for after-the-fact justification.
4. Romance your audience, and they'll love you back. People like people who make them feel good about themselves, and they buy from people they like.
5. Buy their attention with entertainment value. You're asking people to give you something even more valuable than their money—their time. They won't give you either unless you make it worth their while.
6. When you run commercials that consumers like to watch, you don't have to spend extra media dollars airing them so often.

Chapter Two
Numbers vs. Reality

When desktop computers first penetrated business offices in the late 1980s, corporations first thought they'd usher in paperless workplaces. They didn't. That's because managers soon discovered that by manipulating the data stored on hard drives and floppy discs, they could generate all sorts of reports. Not necessarily useful or insightful reports, but impressively thick ones.

Ever since then, business in general, and marketing in particular, have suffered from an overreliance on massive amounts of often meaningless numbers.

With this reliance arose another one–on cadres of button-pushers who knew far more about the often mysterious workings of the hardware and software they served than of the human hearts and minds they were using online technology to talk to and sell to.

Coupled with this was the almost ritualistic belief that relying on numbers to tell you about how your target audience was behaving online would magically enable you to establish deep, meaningful relationships between them and your brand of deodorant.

But while "technology has utterly changed the way consumers get and use information," brand strategist Jonathan Baskin Salem wrote in *Advertising Age*[1],

> . . . smart, earnest people...believe that the new technology has also changed human nature and the very purpose of business function. It did neither. People still need and do the same things they always did, and companies still need to sell to them. Pretending that conversation has any value apart from the meaningful, relevant and useful information within it— ...or that anybody wakes up in the morning hoping to have a conversation with a brand of toothpaste or insurance—is no longer credible..."

Brand Advertising

Online marketing—particularly social network marketing—can get your brand all kinds of likes, shares, friendings and other sorts of impressive numbers. But not necessarily another kind: Sales.

"Every CMO should...pause and reflect...especially if you're about to roll out a social-media campaign," Salem warns. "Unfortunately, there are many reasons why you shouldn't, and may not."

One such reason was Pepsi's 2010 decision to get themselves out of the brand's perennial number-two position (behind Coke) by replacing Super Bowl television advertising with a social networking program instead. This program was built around the idea of the "Refresh Project," in which consumers with "refreshing ideas that change the world" were invited to apply online for a share of $20 million in grant money.

At first, it seemed to be working. Pepsi's announcement that it was bowing out of the Super Bowl attracted more publicity than Coke's two 60-second Super Bowl spots. The Refresh Project generated good relations between local Pepsi bottlers and their communities. The company announced that the Refresh Project was getting an "unbelievable response."

But the only connection between the campaign and the brand it was supposed to be promoting was that it used the verb "Refresh," which is what a cola's supposed to do. The rest was all about idealistic charitable good works, which any brand, for any product category, could have been supporting. Teens and 20somethings, who comprise the bulk of cola drinkers, moreover, aren't exactly famous for their big-time, dedicated charitable commitments.

In a way, the campaign achieved its objective, though not exactly in the way Pepsi hoped. It broke them out of the dreaded number-two spot, all right, by bumping them down to third—behind not only Coke but Diet Coke as well.

From 2004 through 2011, Burger King's advertising agency, Crispin Porter & Bogusky, moved the brand heavily into Facebook campaigns and viral videos. Their campaigns got all kinds of response and engagement, but not so much in the way of sales. Over six consecutive quarters, from second quarter 2009 through third quarter 2010 (the latest quarter reported at the time), BK same-store sales were down. And it wasn't the economy, stupid; while Burger King's estimated 2010 sales were down 2.5% to $8.7 billion, McDonald's sales went up 4.4%, to $32.4 billion. Which is why the client finally fired the agency.

It's bad enough when campaigns like these talk past their intended audiences. But what's even worse is how some data-driven campaigns can alienate them.

In 2011, Ragu created an online video campaign in which wives talked about how clueless their husbands were in the kitchen. Then, to generate buzz (more meaningless numbers), they sent links to it to prominent dad bloggers on Twitter. They too got buzz, in the form of a backlash of posts by prominent dad bloggers about the brand being anti-fatherhood.

As the Arab Spring kicked off in Egypt that year, some button-pusher working for Kenneth Cole shoes noted that #Cairo was trending massively on Twitter. Based on that alone, the brand tweeted, "Millions are in uproar in #Cairo. Rumor is they heard our new spring collection is available online."

In September, 2013, in the midst of serious debate on whether or not to send U. S. troops to deal with poison gas in the Syrian civil war, Cole tweeted, "'Boots on the ground' or not, let's not forget about sandals, pumps and loafers." The tweet went viral, which would make the button-pushers happy, but with so much, and such vehement, negative response that even Cole realized he'd really, er, put his foot in it. He defended his tone-deaf tweeting as "provocative ways to encourage a healthy dialogue about important issues, including HIV/AIDS, war, and homelessness," telling the Daily Mail that "I'm well aware of the risks that come with this approach."

In 2012, when Hurricane Sandy struck East Coast, Allstate was running commercials before the storm telling policyholders how to file claims and American Express was emailing cardholders offering "emergency financial, medical or travel assistance." But other brands, notably retailers, were using trend data showing that the hurricane was a hot topic to demonstrate that those who ignore history are doomed to repeat it.

- Jonathan Adler sent out an e-mail blast inviting consumers to "storm our site" and get free shipping by entering "code Sandy at checkout."
- American Apparel tweeted about a "Hurricane Sandy Sale" for consumers "bored during the storm"—as opposed to those injured or left homeless—with checkout code "Sandysale."

Brand Advertising

- After tweeting pro forma wishes that customers "stay safe," the Gap asked, "We'll be doing lots of Gap.com shopping today. How about you?"
- Urban Outfitters sent out a bad-taste fart pun and offered free shipping with the checkout code "Allsoggy."

Overreliance on numbers can also lead to marketing communication with a tin ear, which, in turn, can lead to disaster.

QUANTAS airlines learned this the expensive way.

Coming off a bitter lockout and a string of safety failures that grounded their whole fleet and stranded passengers around the world in 2011, the Australian international carrier decided that what they needed was a Twitter promotion asking consumers to tweet back their idea of a "dream luxury flight experience" using the hashtag QuantasLuxury.

It wasn't.

The first tweeted response, from one Axel Bruns, said his dream luxury experience would be, "Planes that arrive intact and on time..." It went downhill from there. Stephen Dann said his QANTAS luxury experience would be "Flights that leave on schedule because Management doesn't arbitrarily shut down the airline."

The QANTAS Luxury campaign was totally lacking in common sense. But when you consider who actually does the Twitter promotions and how blinkered their mindsets, you'll see that common sense is all too uncommon. As kiwi_kali tweeted, "Somewhere in Quantas HQ a middle manager is yelling at a Gen Y social media 'expert' to make it all stop. LOL"

And that's the root of the problem.

Too many advertisers turn to vendors or in-house staff who claim expert technical knowledge of the software and the Internet. "It's too true that often company executives, desperate to show that they have a digital strategy, think that forgoing spending money on [an] actual properly planned digital advertising campaign, and instead opting for free and poorly thought-out staff plugs on Twitter, is the way forward," cautions Emma Barnett in the (UK) Telegraph. As a result, she adds, "it is frequently the case that the people in charge of 'social media'...are also very young and inexperienced at traditional marketing—because all things digital are perceived as a young person's area."[2]

Brand Advertising

This perception proved costly to Habitat, the British furniture retail chain.

In 2009, when the Green Revolution in Iran was still going strong, some social media "expert" at Habitat checked out the top ten trending topics and mindlessly decided to paste the top hashtags -- including "Iran" and "Mousavi" -- into promotional tweets.

Never mind that events of far more geopolitical significance than furniture sales were taking place. Never mind that people in Iran and worldwide were using social networking to share information and eyewitness accounts, link to news reports and coordinate protests against the recent rigged election results. They're top topics, so let's use them.

And use them they did, pasting them into hashtags without even knowing what the hashtags referred to, with tweets like: HabitatUK: #MOUSAVI Join the database for free to win a gift card.

The backlash was almost as violent as Ahmadinejad's crackdown, causing Habitat to post that "We were totally shocked when we discovered what happened and are very sorry for the offence [sic] that has been caused."

Alex Burmaster, Nielsen Online communications director, pointed out the one basic truth that eluded Habitat's social media "experts," focused like a laser on trend rankings instead of the real world. "Advertising in social media can be like gatecrashing a party," he noted. "People who use social media are much less tolerant to have their conversations interrupted by advertisers."

This suggests that you'd do better trusting your social-media marketing to people with a knowledge of ways to interrupt people's media use without alienating them.

"Social media has often not been the best way for companies to communicate their brand message," Barnett said with typical British understatement. "It is good for responding to customers, but any marketing, even on social sites, needs the same level of thought, crisis management and craftsmanship as a traditional advertising campaign."

It makes sense to let social media "experts" do the button-pushing and other back-end stuff for your campaign. But unless you're suicidal, it makes absolutely no sense to put them in charge of your marketing strategy and content.

For that, you should trust advertising experts instead of computer "experts."

When you do, the results can be extremely gratifying—to both your brand and your audience.

For example, Procter & Gamble's "the man your man could smell like" YouTube campaign for Old Spice generated tons of response, but even more sales. One reason is that what a man smells like is integral to selling products like a body wash. Another is that it was targeted to women, who do most of the shopping for men's deodorants, after shaves and other toiletries. Third, it at least referenced the Old Spice brand's maritime-related positioning. And the capper, when these women went to their supermarkets to check out Old Spice body wash, they found very attractive promotional pricing.

Ford's Fiesta Movement Facebook campaign, too, produced not only views and likes, but actual leads for dealers. It also produced amazing sales-conversion numbers, because when those leads showed up at dealerships to take test-drives, they found a car whose high quality belied its low pricing.

Numbers are great for telling you who your target audience is and when and where to reach them. But not for what kind of message to reach them with.

The human beings who buy your products have not only eyes and ears, but also minds and hearts—and to an extent some advertisers may not realize, it's the latter that drives purchase decisions.

In the next chapter we look back to a time when a group of people working in advertising seemed to understand this and started a revolution in the business because of it.

Chapter Three
Don't let it be forgot
That once there was a spot
For one brief, shining moment
That was known as Camelot.

In the beginning, there was Volney Palmer. Though history credits him as the first advertising agent, by modern job descriptions he'd be a media rep. Palmer sold space in newspapers he represented to national advertisers, in return for which the papers would give him 15 percent of the price of the space (i.e., billings) as commission.

As the 20th Century began, Francis W. Ayer set up a company he named after his father, N. W. Ayer, to take the process one step farther. At the time, local newspapers were hungry for national advertising revenues and national advertisers were hungry for media to run their ads in, but there was no way to get them together. Local newspaper sales departments didn't know how to reach advertisers' sales managers. And advertisers knew next to nothing about newspapers outside their own local areas; in this pre-phone-book era, their circulations, rates, even names and mailing addresses were deep, dark mysteries. So Ayer put together a national newspaper directory for advertisers. This publication listed newspapers' names, addresses, rates, circulations, etc. The circulation figures weren't audited; in fact, they were closer to wishful thinking, usually being whatever the papers said they were. Acceptance standards for listing in the Ayer Directory were equally rigorous: a newspaper had to agree to pay the N. W. Ayer agency 15 percent of whatever they got paid for carrying non-local advertising on their pages.

By the 1920s, other advertising agencies had sprung up, all serving clients by advising them how and where to place advertising most effectively, but not making the ads themselves. Despite this—or maybe because of it—advertising began to accomplish unprecedentedly amazing things. It persuaded men to shave daily instead of weekly, people to bathe and wash every day instead of just on Saturday night. By giving out the first orange-juice squeezers as premiums, it got people to start consuming oranges in liquid rather than solid form. And with their morning orange juice, it got them to eat cold cereal instead of oatmeal.

Ad-making was done by outside freelancers, the most prominent of whom was Claude Hopkins. Working primarily in direct-response advertising, whose results were measurable, he developed a whole slew of principles, many of which are still valid today. He believed that advertising should be built around consumer benefit (what's in it for me?), which would trump product attribute (it's smoother) every time. He believed that headlines could and should be written to target the right audience in a mass medium. He believed that strong specifics were worth much more than weak generalities, particularly when those specifics could be marshaled to support benefit claims with reasons why. He believed that visuals, though potentially wasteful because they took up lots of space on the page, if used at all should convey sales points. He believed in creating what we today call brand personality, and in maintaining that personality through ad-after-ad consistency. "Doing admirable things in a different way," he wrote, gives a brand "an individuality best suited to the people [it] addresses." He believed in creating advertising strategies before making ads, and though he kept harping on avoiding things that waste money by making ads too big, he was a firm believer in production values. The costs of investing in quality production, he said, were mere fractions of the costs of media insertion. And finally, he believed in the Lean Production principle of free and complete sharing of knowledge, writing that "An ad-writer, to have a chance at success, must gain full information on his subject."

So far, so good. But Hopkins believed in a lot of garbage, too. Most of it came from one big, false premise—that scientific management could be applied to advertising. He even wrote a famous book called *Scientific Advertising*, a title as oxymoronic as jumbo shrimp or democratic socialism. "The time has come," his book began, "when advertising has in some hands reached the status of a science. It is based on fixed principles and is reasonably exact." These "fixed principles" were presumably based on research techniques, such as ad testing and tracking, headline testing and test-marketing, which Hopkins either espoused or invented. But boy, did they lead to some wacky conclusions.

Since advertising was salesmanship, Hopkins said, and since people didn't like unusual-looking salesman, ads really shouldn't look very different from average. Headlines shouldn't be too big. Aside from wasting precious space, a large headline would be like a salesman shouting. Body copy shouldn't be larger than eight-point type for the same reason. Of course, a four-city Newspaper Advertising Bureau study in the mid-1980s was to show that nearly one-third of people over 65 have trouble reading newspapers in ten-point type, but maybe there weren't so many old geezers alive and kicking in Hopkins's heyday. And he believed in not singling out key sales points, but in telling what he called the full story—easy enough to do in eight-point body copy, but try pulling it off in a 30-second television commercial running in a six-spot pod, with research showing that you're lucky if consumers absorb 1.25 ideas in a half-minute.

By the 1930s, advertising agencies had taken the creation of ads in-house, and much of the Hopkins philosophy along with it. Particularly the testing part. Since more and more advertising called for consumers to buy something at the store instead of sending a coupon with an order, the leading agencies of the time developed research techniques to measure the factors that increased ad readership.

Young & Rubicam, for example, commissioned a young social scientist named George Gallup to give them the basis of a formula that would increase their clients' ads' readership. The formula that resulted called for four-color ads with large and subsidiary visuals. The research found that men liked to look at pictures of men, women at pictures of women, and both at pictures of babies. Headlines of an optimal number of words needed to be supplemented with subheads. The way to get more readers to actually read the body copy was to break it up into bite-size chunks, either laying out the ad picture-and-caption style, or, if the copy was too long for that, breaking it up with crossheads. The copy itself should be set in a serif font and should be justified (flush left and right, like this book).

Not very surprisingly, as word of this formula began to seep out, ads industry-wide began to take on a formulaic appearance. David Ogilvy, who'd worked for George Gallup, went on to found an agency whose print work essentially followed the formula into the '70s. But by the 1960s, other agencies were trying different ways to stand out by breaking it.

In Chicago, Leo Burnett was introducing "critters," illustrated and animated characters to personify his clients' packaged goods—the Jolly

Green Giant for Green Giant canned vegetables; Snap, Crackle and Pop for Kellogg's Rice Krispies and Tony the Tiger for Frosted Flakes; the Pillsbury dough boy; elves living in a tree for Keebler crackers. The most famous Burnett critter, though, was a flesh-and-blood, live-action one—the Marlboro cowboy, who had the power to rejuvenate a failing brand of women's cigarettes by giving it a sex change, to reshape American habits by persuading consumers that real men did smoke filter cigarettes, and to endure as an effective campaign for nearly half a century.

In New York at Ted Bates, Rosser Reeves was developing the idea of the Unique Selling Proposition, which would differentiate a client's commodity-like package good from its almost identical competition, especially if the USP was repeated three times, as in "Anacin—for fast, fast, fast relief" or "Certs—it's two, two, two mints in one."

But not far from Bates, in a set of dumpy offices across West 42nd Street from the main branch of the New York Public Library, an agency opened which permanently changed the face of the advertising industry—one which seemed to revolutionize the business from top to bottom, but in fact did it only part way. The agency was Doyle Dane Bernbach, which is notable for not only the way it permanently changed the face of advertising, but for the way it created a structure which virtually all agencies follow to this day. Like all revolutions, it started with a vision—a vision with a lot of Lean Production overtones to it, enunciated by Bill Bernbach in 1947, two years before DDB opened its doors, and about six years before DDB's work started to attract notice. From an internal memo Bernbach wrote while still creative director at Grey Advertising, it's clear he wasn't exactly a big fan of scientific advertising:

> There are a lot of great technicians in advertising. And unfortunately, they talk the best game. They know all the rules. They can tell you that people in an ad will get you greater readership. They can tell you that a sentence should be this short or that long. They can tell you that body copy should be broken up for easier and more inviting reading. They can give you fact after fact after fact. They are the scientists of advertising. But there's one little rub. Advertising

is fundamentally persuasion, and persuasion happens to be not a science, but an art.

All this is not to say that technique is unimportant. Superior technical skill will make a good man better. But the danger is a preoccupation with technical skill or the mistaking of technical skill for creative ability.[2]

A company will spend years in research and hundreds of thousands of dollars [more like half-millions of today's dollars] to create a point of difference for its product, and then use run-of-the-mill advertising to convey that difference to the people. Why? They must know that if their ad looks and sounds like all the others, their product will be classed with all the others. So often the words are saying, "Look how different I am" while the total ad says, "Pay no attention to me, I'm really one of the boys."[3]

In 1960, when Doyle Dane (as it was known to people outside the industry; New York ad people called it either "DDB" or just "Doyle") was eleven years old and the agency to beat, he went further. Remember what Hopkins said about ads needing to look average because people expected salesmen to? And that all the product differentiation should be in the headline and eight-point body copy? Bernbach begged to differ:

And by then, he knew what he was talking about. His agency was in the process of turning a cramped, uncomfortable, obsolete (designed in the 1930s by Ferdinand Porsche), ugly little foreign car into a runaway best seller and reverse status symbol, while growing billings from $25 million to $270 million (from around $132 million to $2.2 billion in today's dollars) in a decade.

What's amazing about the DDB creative revolution was not that it threw out many of Hopkins's scientific advertising laws, but that it kept so many, with nobody being the wiser.

Hopkins believed in creating brand personalities, personalities made an emotional connection with prospective customers. DDB created them – for Volkswagen, for Avis car rental, for Polaroid cameras, for Levy's Rye Bread, for Mobil gasoline.

Hopkins believed in being factual and telling the full story. So did DDB (at least in print media), to the point that their copy, amazingly, was far heavier on attributes and features than benefits.

Brand Advertising

Take a look at the complete copy of the famous "Lemon" VW ad. We defy you to find one explicitly stated benefit before the final sentence of its beautifully written body copy (big enough to read on the next page).

Lemon.

This Volkswagen missed the boat. The chrome strip on the glove compartment is blemished and must be replaced. Chances are you wouldn't have noticed it; Inspector Kurt Kroner did.

There are 3,389 men at our Wolfsburg factory with only one job: to inspect Volkswagens at each stage of production. (3000 Volkswagens are produced daily; there are more inspectors than cars.)

Every shock absorber is tested (spot checking won't do), every windshield is scanned. VWs have been rejected for surface scratches barely visible to the eye.

Final inspection is really something! VW inspectors run each car off the line onto the Funktionsprüfstand (car test stand), tote up 189 check points, gun ahead to the automatic brake stand, and say "no" to one VW out of fifty.

This preoccupation with detail means the VW lasts longer and requires less maintenance, by and large, than other cars. (It also means a used VW depreciates less than any other car.)

We pluck the lemons; you get the plums.

This Volkswagen missed the boat.

The chrome strip on the glove compartment is blemished and must be replaced. Chances are you wouldn't have noticed it. Inspector Kurt Kramer did.

There are 3,389 men at our Wolfsburg factory with only one job: to inspect Volkswagens at each stage of production. (3000 Volkswagens are produced daily; there are more inspectors than cars.)

Every shock absorber is tested (spot checking won't do), every windshield is scanned. VWs have been rejected for surface scratches barely visible to the eye.

Final inspection is really something! VW inspectors run each car off the line onto the Funktionsprufstand (car-test stand), tote up 189 check points, gun ahead to the automatic brake stand, and say "no" to one VW out of fifty.

This preoccupation with detail means the VW lasts longer and requires less maintenance, by and large, than other cars. (It also means a used VW depreciates less than any other car.)

Same with the defining ad of another DDB signature campaign, for Avis:

> Avis is only No. 2 in rent a cars.
> So why go with us?
>
> We try harder.
> (When you're not the biggest, you have to.)
> We just can't afford dirty ashtrays. Or half-empty gas tanks. Or worn wipers. Or unwashed cars. Or low tires. Or anything less than seat-adjusters that adjust. Heaters that heat. Defrosters that defrost.
> Obviously, the thing we try hardest for is just to be nice. To start you out right with a new car, like a lively, super-torque Ford, and a pleasant smile. To know, say, where you get a good pastrami sandwich in Duluth.
> Why?
> Because we can't afford to take you for granted.
> Go with us next time.
> The line at our counter is shorter.

Brand Advertising

Avis is only No.2 in rent a cars. So why go with us?

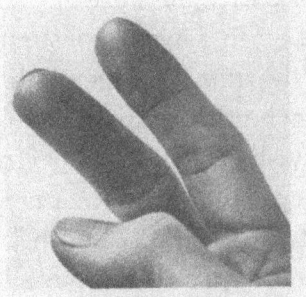

We try harder.
(When you're not the biggest, you have to.)
We just can't afford dirty ashtrays. Or half-empty gas tanks. Or worn wipers. Or unwashed cars. Or low tires. Or anything less than seat-adjusters that adjust. Heaters that heat. Defrosters that defrost.

Obviously, the thing we try hardest for is just to be nice. To start you out right with a new car, like a lively, super-torque Ford, and a pleasant smile. To know, say, where you get a good pastrami sandwich in Duluth.

Why?

Because we can't afford to take you for granted.

Go with us next time.

The line at our counter is shorter.

©1963 AVIS, INC.

Someone at Doyle must obviously have believed in Hopkins's rule (and also the Lean Production principle) of making all the information available, because the ads are filled with it.

And that same someone was probably a big believer, along with Hopkins, in getting the strategy first. Legend has it that the Avis Number

2 campaign came about because Bernbach got his best people to work on the account by promising them that he'd sell whatever they came up with—and that all they could honestly come up with was that Avis was number 2 in car rental volume and that they were going to try harder. But there's much more to it than that. At the time, Avis was a very distant second to Hertz and was pulling out all the stops to keep close-third National from nipping at their heels. The Number 2 campaign aroused underdog sympathies by making it seem as if Avis was closing in on Hertz—which left poor National in the dust.

Their Levy's Jewish Rye Bread campaign is also far more deviously strategic (and we intend that as a compliment) than it looks. Levy's was a regional brand sold in and around New York City. Because it was a Jewish-style rye, Levy's originally marketed it to Jewish consumers, advertising it primarily in the *New York Post*, at the time the paper with the city's largest Jewish readership (except for maybe the Yiddish-language *Jewish Daily Forward*). The problem was that Jewish consumers knew from Jewish rye—and compared to the rye bread they could get in their neighborhood Jewish bakeries (which were almost as plentiful back then as neighborhood pizzerias are today), mass-produced, packaged Levy's Rye just didn't cut it (kind of like the difference between pizzeria pizza and frozen pizza). So DDB came up with the strategy of selling Levy's rye bread to non-Jews as a Jewish delicacy. To this end, they switched media placement to the *New York Daily News* (the big general-population, blue-collar paper) and to subway-platform posters. The executions were right on strategy, showing an obviously Irish cop, a Chinese waiter, an Italian altar boy, etc., enjoying a sandwich on Levy's rye under the headline, "You don't have to be Jewish to love Levy's." In fact, it helped if you weren't, as Levy's sales curves soon showed.

Executionally, DDB set the established look of advertising on its head. In an interview many years after the fact, art director Helmut Krone said he created the Volkswagen campaign's look by taking the design formula for most advertising of the time and deliberately doing the opposite. Instead of color, he used black-and-white. Instead of illustration exaggerating desired product attributes, he used starkly realistic photography. Instead of showing people in his photos to attract readership, his visuals were dominated by the product. In sharp contrast to Hopkins's scientific

Lean Advertising

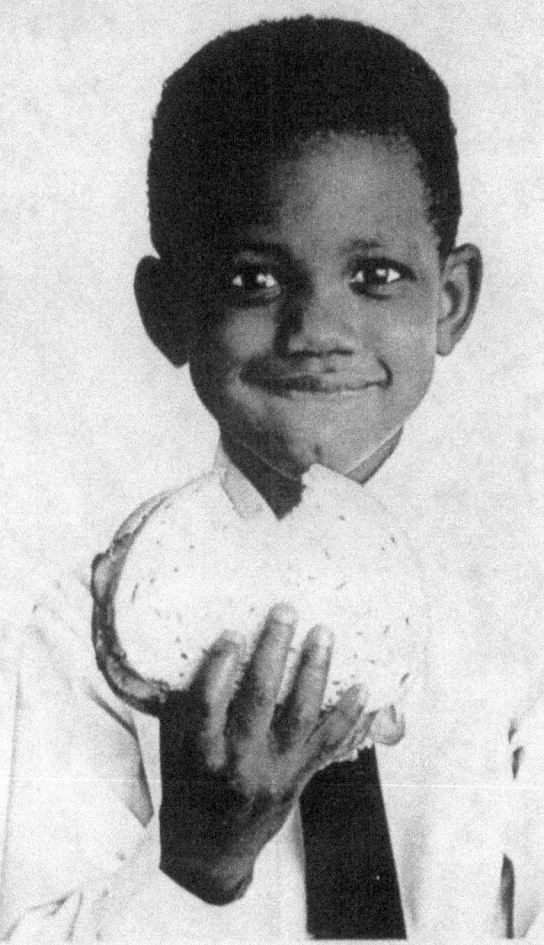

Brand Advertising

Lean Advertising

rules, the photo took up the top two-thirds of the page. Body copy was necessarily shorter. It was also sans serif. Paragraphs were still justified, but they were set in narrower columns. Some had one-word widows. Other paragraphs were a total of one or two words long in their entirety. Two years later, when the Volkswagen look had become an industry norm, he once again stood the prevailing look on its head, this time for Avis. Here, he said, he went from big visual to small, and from normal to large type, even for body copy.

The old "scientific advertising" formula look.

Brand Advertising

DDB stood it on its head...

No. 2ism.
The Avis Manifesto.

We are in the rent a car business, playing second fiddle to a giant.

Above all, we've had to learn how to stay alive.

In the struggle, we've also learned the basic difference between the No.1's and No.2's of the world.

The No.1 attitude is: "Don't do the wrong thing. Don't make mistakes and you'll be O.K."

The No.2 attitude is: "Do the right thing. Look for new ways. Try harder."

No. 2ism is the Avis doctrine. And it works.

The Avis customer rents a clean, new Plymouth, with wipers wiping, ashtrays empty, gas tank full, from an Avis girl with smile firmly in place.

And Avis itself has come out of the red into the black.

Avis didn't invent No. 2ism. Anyone is free to use it.

No. 2's of the world, arise!

...and stood it on its head again.

Bill Bernbach's agency revolutionized not only ads, but the structure which produced them. Before DDB, ads were done by "slide-it-under-the-door" art direction. The copywriter would get his assignment from the account executive, write the copy, revise it for AE and then client approval. Then the approved finished copy would be handed to an "artist" or "layout man" who would lay out the page, deciding which elements went where, specifying the type and supervising the illustration or photography and the pasteup. At no time did the writer and "artist" ever work together. Until DDB, that is. By creating copywriter/art director teams, Bernbach more than doubled the brain power that could be applied to an ad. Not only were two people working on the overall idea, but their specialties interacted. Skip back to a few pages, and you'll see how the Volkswagen layout design influenced the writing style. But more than that, previously unheard-of things would happen, like writers coming up with visual ideas, or art directors writing great headlines, or one team member's idea triggering a better idea from the other.

This structure, with copywriter/art director teams making up a creative department, is the one that virtually all advertising agencies followed until recently. But now it's likely to be found only in larger, established, multi-media agencies. With the rise of the Internet and the decline of traditional media, numbers have re-emerged with a vengeance and the old-time Hopkins "Scientific Advertising" theories have come back. The goal of persuasion and conntecting emotionally with prospective customers has been forgotten by many smaller, so-called "digital" firms. In outfits such as these, art directors have largely gone the way of the dinosaur to be replaced by graphic artists who may reside halfway around the world from the person who actually wrote the words.

Nevertheless, there's no question that Doyle Dane Bernbach was a revolutionary advertising agency and the biggest and that the best still follow the DDB copywriter / art director team model. But there is question as to whether or not DDB's revolution was a Lean one. In some ways it was, but in more ways it was counterrevolutionary.

Let's look at some of the internal characteristics of Lean Production to see which was which.

First, Lean Production begins with a vision, supported by consistent top-management action, of what the organization will become. Bill

Bernbach certainly had such a vision, and he supported it. He had a winning attitude and was able to instill this in subordinates. "We must develop our own philosophy and not have the advertising philosophy of others imposed on us," he wrote. "Let us prove to the world that good taste, good art, good writing can be good selling."

Second, everyone in the organization has a championship-team mentality and esprit de corps. Everyone at DDB did—well into the 1970s, when the justification for it, along with Bill Bernbach's edge, had ceased to exist.

Third, the organization breaks down walls. DDB broke down some walls while erecting others. They broke down the socioeconomic barriers that kept lower-class non-WASPs out of advertising. By way of contrast, when Bruce Goldman held down his first advertising job at Young & Rubicam in the early '60s, he and his fellow summer copy trainees had been recruited through the colleges they went to—Yale, Princeton, Columbia and, because a client's son went there, non-Ivy-League Stanford.

As the book *When Advertising Tried Harder* describes, DDB broke down the barriers between writing and art direction, and between both and the client:

> By merging the two disciplines of copy and art direction into one creative function—the "creative department"—the structure of most ad agencies was forever altered. The change was more than physical: it was also philosophical. Artists and writers were brought out of the back room, the leash was removed, and direct contact with the client not only was permitted, it was encouraged. Lines of communication were shortened. Less seemed to be lost in translation. The creative department was able to fight for its own ideas, to sell them and produce them.[4]

Creating creative teams helped accomplish—but only partially—the Lean Production objective of pushing decision-making down to the people who actually did the work, who were probably in better position to recognize what needed to be done in a given situation because they were right there on the spot. Creative teams were "empowered" to decide on the best course of action and take it. They were encouraged to think outside the box—not, in true Lean Production style, about how processes can be improved and what changes should be implemented, but about how to make the resulting work, performed through revolutionized but existing processes, better. Over time, writers and art directors learned how to function as team players, at least with each other, going through the four stages typical of Lean Production team formation.

We'll call stage one "Forming." It's marked by uncertainty and distance between members, by feeling unsure about roles and relationships. Think of it as the "getting acquainted" part of a team's life cycle.

The next stage, called "Norming," occurs when the team begins to settle down and become an efficient unit from which predictable patterns emerge and a style of work develops.

"Storming," which happens next, is what typically results when conflicts arise. This is the critical stage, in which perseverance is crucial. At advertising agencies in the '60s, this was known as closing the door and letting the bodies bounce off the wall until you both came out with a great idea.

The final, fruitful stage is "Performing," when a mature team can be counted on to deliver solutions. "Performing" often is at its most spectacular in high-pressure situations, on tight deadlines, or under conditions that may require superhuman effort. Top-performing teams can create amazing results. And if you don't believe that from the work that DDB created in the '60s, then download the movie, *Apollo 13*, and see what such a process looked like.

But while the DDB revolution tore down some walls, it erected others, mainly between the creative department and everyone else. It also made an existing wall higher. Traffic departments, whose function had been to manage the work flow, now took on the added role of buffering the creatives from time and people pressures that would otherwise force them to expose good work before its time.

A fourth internal characteristic of Lean Producers is universal realization that mundane tasks are absolutely necessary and must be executed with care and efficiency. They must be carried out professionally because, as in the case of a masterpiece, the smallest tasks combine to create the whole. At DDB, art directors were famous (or maybe infamous) for cutting apart type proofs, letter by letter, to get precisely the right letter spacing on finished mechanicals. Copywriter, later copy supervisor, Jack

Dillon used to write by putting a page of paper in his typewriter, typing a sentence, removing the paper, and then repeating the process until it was time to sort through a whole stack of paper, comparing variations of sentences and their order. Though not at DDB at the time, Amil Gargano, who'd go on to become a principal of Ally Gargano, would order photostats of each element of an ad in about a dozen different sizes, then spend days playing mix-and-match to arrive at the best possible permutation.

Lean Agencies, like other Lean Producers, realize that quality must be built in and can never be inspected in after the fact. When it came to producing ads, DDB creative teams' meticulous attention to even mundane tasks like body copy and mechanicals built quality in. But as the agency grew with success, it set up a hierarchy to inspect quality into concepts; concepts had to go through copy and art supervisors, sometimes through the copy chief and head art director, through Mr. Bernbach himself if the project were major enough, and then on to the client. (Bruce Goldman remembers one instance from the mid-1970s when this approach proved disastrous to a campaign for the Israel Government Tourist Office. It was the time of the first wave of Palestinian terror bombings in Israel, and American Jews—a major source of tourism dollars—were understandably reluctant to vacation there. To offset this sales resistance, he came up with the campaign line, "Part of you is already here." Before going to the client, the campaign had to first be submitted to Mr. Bernbach, who looked and it and said, "Oh, you mean you'll find another piece of yourself." Undeterred by what that wording might mean in light of the violence and its potential effects on detonees, Bernbach kept repeating that the campaign to presented should be, "Find another piece of yourself." And when it was presented to the Israeli clients that way, they said, "Sure! You'll find your arm over here and your leg over there..." and killed the campaign.)

Lean Producers work tirelessly and relentlessly to eliminate anything in the process which doesn't add value. One thing that DDB eliminated was the tightly rendered layouts of ad concepts which other agencies of the time considered essential to sell the client. These were time-consuming and expensive to produce, and most clients were too smart to be swayed by the packaging alone. Instead, DDB presented its work in marker roughs—just tight enough to read the headlines, figure out what the visuals were and deduce the relationship between them. Not only did this avoid expense and delay, but it avoided quibbles over irrelevancies like the way a person was drawn or the specific type face. Once, in the aftermath of the 1973 oil embargo, when DDB presented a rough of an ad with a man pointing a gas-pump nozzle to his head above the headline "Or get a Volkswagen," the client even insisted on using art director Charles Piccirillo's rough drawing in the final ad instead of the work of a professional cartoonist.

Finally, people working for a Lean Producer are all driven by a higher motivation than doing their specific jobs. An engineer at a Lean company, for example, may get paid for designing circuit boards. He may even have the title, Chief Engineer, Computer Memory Chip Division. But more likely, he'd see himself as a member of a team dedicated to "serving the community by providing products and services of superior quality at a fair price." Likewise, a Wal-Mart employee who's bought into what the company is about will not define himself or herself as a checkout clerk, but as someone with the worthier job of "providing value to our customers,"[5] just as the Nordstrom sales representative may see his role as offering "service to the customer above all else."[6] If the authors of the best-selling book, *Built to Last*, are correct, a Sony product manager may see herself as being engaged in a worthwhile struggle "to elevate the Japanese culture and national status"[7] and the Walt Disney worker as being part of an effort to "bring happiness to millions."[8]

Workers in a Lean Enterprise, from the top of the organization to the bottom, know what they they stand for because they know what the group they belong to stands for. It's the very reason they're in business. This may be the single most important factor in the success of market leaders in general, no matter in what industry they operate. According to the authors of *Built to Last*,[9] the right culture may be more important than superb products, or good ideas, or technological innovation. They theorize that these companies have come to dominate their industries because their employees know that they exist to produce products and services that make useful and important contributions to the lives of customers. Indeed, great products are not what make the organization outstanding. It's the other way around. The organization is what creates great products.

Doyle Dane Bernbach came to dominate its industry through good ideas and superior products. But to them (and their spinoffs, followers and imitators), that was as far as the vision went. It was a dedication first to advancing the state of the art, and then only consequently to contributing to their customers. Its ads were great products which made the organization outstanding, not the other way around. It was fanatical about improving the work but indifferent, after one major structural change had been accomplished, to improving the process which produced it. And it was oblivious to the need to eliminate all the non-value-adding, time-and-money-wasting ways of doing business that eventually turn revolutions into business-as-usual.

The time has come for an agency structure that will complete, extend and sustain the revolution Doyle Dane Bernbach started in traditional multi-media agencies. It's also time for many digital agencies to realize what they sacrifice by taking their eyes off the ball of persuasion and emotional connectivity while instead keeping them so firmly fixed on likes, click-throughs, and page views.

Chapter Four
Many hands vs. too many cooks

Remember the Volkswagen ad copy from the previous chapter? Remember how proud VW was that it had more inspectors than cars? That their defect rate was only one in 50 cars? (On a daily run of 3,000, that would mean 60 rejects.) Well, Toyota turns out substantially more cars per day. Without a single quality inspector. They reserve ten parking spaces for defective cars, and if any day those spaces get filled, they shut down the line to fix whatever's causing the defects.

That's the paradigm for the difference between a Doyle Dane Bernbach-style advertising agency (and virtually all agencies today are DDB-style agencies) and a Lean Agency.

Yes, agencies have slimmed down some. But only some.

Yes, the staff-to-billings ratio has gone down from ten people per million dollars' billings in the 1960s to less than one per million today. But that's more the result of inflation and computerization than of any intentional leanness on the agencies' part.

According to the Bureau of Labor Statistics' Consumer Price Indices, it would take $7.22 in 2016 currency to get you what a dollar could buy in 1967. Heck, it takes more than four million bucks today to buy just 30 seconds' worth of air time on the Super Bowl.

And yes, a whole bunch of jobs have been computerized out of existence. Copy typists don't type and retype copy anymore; copywriters word-process it. Type directors don't specify type anymore; art directors spec and set it with QuarkXpress or InDesign. Secretaries don't answer phones and take messages anymore; voicemail systems do. That's all well and good, but it's far from Lean.

Traffic departments, which are supposed to smooth and speed the flow of work, can often impede it. Just doing the paperwork to open a job can set it back a day or two and cost the client a few hundred dollars—with just a filled-out job order form to show for the time and money.

But if you think that's wasteful, how about the layer upon layer upon layer of people in place just to make sure that all the competent, talented people in the agency are doing their jobs right?

Hierarchies are at least as old as the Bible. In the book of Exodus,

Moses's father-in-law, Jethro, drops by for a visit and is distressed to see his son-in-law spending the live-long day, "from morning to evening," teaching the Law to the people and settling their disputes with no help from anyone. So at Jethro's suggestion, Moses sets up what might be the first recorded hierarchy: "leaders of thousands, leaders of hundreds, leaders of fifties and leaders of tens." This hierarchy took the burden of judging—especially the petty cases—off Moses's shoulders and freed him up for very important higher duties.[10] But with the population of the Israelites being about 600,000 at the time, that hierarchy added up to 78,600 functionaries, or more than an eighth (13.1 percent) of the male population (women weren't eligible). Now, when your main missions are teaching and learning an important new set of Laws, gathering manna and building the Tabernacle, and you've got 40 years to accomplish them, being top-heavy isn't all that bad. But for getting things done at a 21st Century pace, it can be deadly.

Bruce Goldman worked at Y&R during both the '60s and the '70s, and though the job titles changed a bit, the number of people that ads had to go through to get approved remained excruciating: first a copy supervisor (later called a creative supervisor), then an associate creative director, the creative director and, for major campaigns, a creative review board. Plus various assistant account executives, account executives, account supervisors and management supervisors along the way. Human nature being what it is, each of these people saw their job as personally changing the work to "improve" it, so no wonder so many fine Arabian stallions got changed into camels. (By the 1990s, the nomenclature had changed again, but not the structure; now it was creative directors, group creative directors, the executive creative director and the chief creative officer.) At Marsteller, where Goldman was a group creative director, he was the second level that work had to go through: first an associate creative director, then a group creative director, then the executive creative director, and then the general manager of the New York office, with assorted account service people putting in their two cents' worth all along the way. Media, account service, production and other departments had similar hierarchies. This quality control system controlled quality, all right—by making sure that very little of it ended up in the clients' advertising. It wasn't until Goldman left New York for Florida and then Richmond that he saw agency structures flatten out—and then because of overall size and budget constraints rather than any commitment to leanness. Steve Martin, after working first at a growing agency in Baltimore and then co-founding the Richmond agency which bears his surname, saw the opposite happen out in what was then the hinterlands—small, flat agencies transforming themselves into Fat, hierarchical ones as they grew.

Not only does the presence of level upon level of supernumeraries in an agency make creating advertising more expensive, not only does it introduce stops, starts and redos (what engineers call "iteration loops") into what should be a continuous process, but it also has the paradoxical effect of making the work worse, not better—by preventing the people who make and place the ads from developing the most effective quality tool there is: individual responsibility.

So do many so-called support functions. Back in the days when there were type directors, many art directors used them as a crutch to avoid thinking very much about type; they'd just pick a font and specify the type as "set to fit." The safety-net of proofreaders can encourage copywriters to get lax and careless as their words go into production. Art directors who can hand off their tissues or rough files to assistants or studio artists for mechanicals forgo the ability to make the fine distinctions between just fitting an ad to the space unit and making it really leap out from the page and grab readers' attention.

In the 1970s, when Goldman worked at Scali McCabe Sloves, copy was still being set in metal type, and the typesetting machines would often break letters. One day, after he signed off on a set of Volvo ad proofs without marking the broken letters for correction, Ed McCabe came storming into his office.

"Why did you sign that this copy was correct when it wasn't," McCabe demanded. "There's a broken letter here, and a broken letter here, and a broken letter here, and you didn't mark them."

"But Ed," Goldman said, "Rich [the production manager] checks for broken letters."

"No," McCabe replied. "Here everyone checks for everything, 'cause the surest way to have things go wrong is to assume the other guy's going to fix them. When it's someone else's responsibility, it ends up as no one's responsibility."

It was a lesson Goldman never forgot—and many advertising agencies never learned.

If the paradigm of Fat Agencies is, "Too many cooks spoil the broth," then the paradigm of Lean Agencies is, "Many hands make light work." The Lean Agency is heavy on people who do the work and light on functionaries whose job it is to critique it—and equally light on standardized measurement, accountability, quality-control and other "best practices" structures. This is because structure doesn't create strong ads, any more than measurement and control create improvement.

The Fat Agency's focus on structure and control is not based on power-madness, but on a sincere, though misguided, desire to make the work better for the client. It's misguided because it sees the work as a sequence of finite, defined, followed, measured steps, usually in different functions, which, if each individually executed by the book, will result in a superior product. This is fine if the steps are things like screwing the rumble-seat hinges onto the body of a Model T Ford, but not so great if any actual thinking needs to be involved. In the 1970s, Edward de Bono, a British physician who devoted his career to the study of how human beings (in all lines of endeavor) come up with creative ideas, published some of his findings in a book called *Lateral Thinking*.[11] Like Fat Producers and Fat Agencies, he wrote, society in general has a strong bias favoring the step-by-step approach, in the belief that the preferred (perhaps the only) way to get from Step A to Step Z is to proceed logically to Steps B, C, D, and so on, in sequence. But that wasn't how it worked in real life, he found. Somewhere around Step B or C, creative thinkers (most of his examples were scientists, who you'd think would be particularly logical) would make what de Bono called an intuitive leap to Step Z, then build a bridge of logic behind them, connecting their intuitive conclusion back to their jumping-off step.

Control structures don't let this happen. They encourage step-by-step-by-step compliance from those below and criticism from those on top, which is not the same as excellence. In fact, this focus on administrative excellence is the enemy of excellence in the work itself. At best, if all the constant controls, critiques and revisions don't eviscerate quality from what's eventually presented to the client, they delay when the client gets to see it (and raise its ultimate cost).

This is why, for example, the Malcolm Baldrige National Quality Award has contributed substantially less to improving the quality of goods and services than has the widespread adoption of Lean Production; because the Baldrige Award criteria focused on procedures, measurements and documentation rather than on creating brilliant products that delight customers.

What a company values shapes the way it works. (An old joke which made the rounds of the New York advertising community in the 1960s illustrated this point. In it, a client's marketing director is looking for an advertising agency and checks out four: J. Walter Thompson, known at the time for seeing client service as servility; McCann-Ericson, known for slavish devotion to research; Young & Rubicam, which had, with its Gallup-formula ads, been a creative hot shop until Doyle Dane Bernbach came along; and DDB itself. The marketing director first visits Thompson and, in the middle of their presentation, asks, "What time is it?" The presenter from Thompson answers, "What time do you want it to be?" Next visit is McCann, where the same question gets, "Let me find out from Research." When the marketing director asks Y&R what time it is, they say, "Let us talk it over with Creative." And at DDB, they tell him, "Look at your own watch, stupid!")

To advertising agency heads who value control, predictability and compliance, a Toyota-like Lean Agency appears the very embodiment of chaos. This is because a Lean Agency runs not as a series of steps, but rather as an overall creative environment. The Lean Agency welcomes chaos and uncertainty as growth media for creativity in all aspects of marketing. Fat Agencies don't, because by definition you can't plan chaos and uncertainty into a control structure. One reason—maybe the major reason—why the Doyle Dane Bernbach structure made traffic departments buffers between creative teams and deadlines was the hope that longer lead times would provide breathing space for the uncertainty that creativity depends on to grow and flourish.

Lean Agency teams will encounter failures from time to time, but failure is tolerated, even expected; if you don't fail every now and then, that means you're not trying. Failure is okay as long as it's an interesting failure, as long as you recognize it in time and as long as you learn from it and go on to build better marketing for the client. This is why a Lean

Agency's biggest potential downside is inconsistency. (Even so, you get more consistency from everyone working on everything than you do from a lot of pigeonholed people each working on a piece of a piece of the business.) Fat Agencies abhor inconsistency as nature abhors a vacuum. Their goal is to turn out work that's safely predictable. (Of course, safely predictable work has a way of becoming stale and repetitious over time. This is why Fat Agencies can lose talented but bored people and clients can become restless, to the point of asking for new teams within the agency or shopping around for new agencies. *BusinessWeek* reports that many are, noting a turn away from mega-agencies to smaller independents "as clients clamor for greater creativity and less bureaucracy.")[12]

In contrast, the Lean Agency team's constant questioning of how to improve both the work and the work process keeps staleness from setting in. Safe and predictable are not characteristics of advertising that gets high readership or viewership and generates disproportionately high ROIs in the marketplace, but, hey, they look great on the PERT chart. This is why a Fat Agency's biggest potential downside is consistent mediocrity.

Fat Agencies treat creation as a straight-line process; the Lean Agency realizes it isn't. Fat Agencies are transactional, Lean Agencies reactional. Fat Agencies are task-based; the Lean Agency is responsibility-based.

	FAT AGENCY	**LEAN AGENCY**
Driving force	Structure	Performance
Main focus	Planning & control	Doing & learning
Evaluation by	Tasks completed	Results achieved
Reviews of	Reports	Concepts/ strategies/ media plans, etc.
Rewards based on	Compliance	Expertise/ achievement
Improvement focus	Task performance, system compliance	Learning curve
Upside	Consistency	Leadership
Downside	Mediocrity	Inconsistency

While Fat Agencies focus on how efficiently each individual step is carried out, the Lean Agency focuses on the overall process and results—how well the work is flowing to the client. Fat Agencies run on structure and control, while the Lean Agency builds expertise and performance.

So while Fat Agencies criticize the work and never question the system, the Lean Agency constantly questions not only the work, but also the system which produces it, constantly looking for ways to improve both. In Fat Agencies, management pushes standards, processes, timetables, etc., down to the workers to make sure they comply with predefined performance criteria. The Lean Agency's bottom-up environment pulls superior performance out of its workers. A Lean Agency doesn't use project-wide task/time-based planning systems; it decentralizes the planning to the people actually doing the work. A Lean Agency doesn't impose standard processes or companywide, top-down philosophies; it just expects its people to know what to do. A Fat Agency requires employees to follow procedures; a Lean Agency expects its people to learn from experience what works and what doesn't.

And to help this happen, a Lean Agency, instead of doling out information like the CIA, on a need-to-know basis, opens complete records of past successes—and failures—to everyone.

The Fat Agency defines campaign direction from the top and then tests the work extensively, revising it according to test finding after test finding, testing the revised work, revising it again, and so on. The Lean Agency builds a series of possibilities for the campaign from the ground up and lets the direction develop as the work does. Its teams pursue lots of different directions, learn a lot from them for decision-making, but test as little as possible, and then only for verification.

A Fat Agency enforces communication through memos, status reports, e-mails and endless meetings. Lean Agency communication is a natural outgrowth of the environment. Fat Agency structure forces individual behavior. In a Lean Agency, leaders pull performance from the people. Fat Agency employees are motivated to please their bosses, Lean Agency workers to surpass their own, and their team's, standards of excellence.

Other than a Toyota, the best way to visualize what a Lean Agency is like is to think of a large, successful winery. There's an administrative staff to keep the books, cut the paychecks, pay the payables and receive the receivables. There are functional groups that take care of the barrels, the bottles, the harvesting, the marketing. There are outside suppliers, like coopers and vineyards. And then there's the winemaker. Nobody reports to the winemaker, but it's his or her wine. Even though it's Nature which sets the growing and harvesting schedule and generally changes it each year, under the winemaker's leadership firm dates for crushing, racking, bottling, exhibiting at key wine shows and shipping are always met. It's the winemaker alone who makes the decisions on which grapes go into the connoisseur brands, which to the winery's regular brand and which will be blended for jug wine. A good winemaker carefully oversees every part of the process through personal observation, not with status reports and administrative reviews. And while everyone in the process is already experienced, each learns more and better techniques each year, and their performance is measured strictly by how much value they contribute to the end product.

Similarly, each new Toyota model is created by a team which a chief engineer leads. Think of him (and since this is a Japanese company we're talking about, it *will* be "him") as an automotive winemaker. It's his vehicle. He makes all the technical decisions, but people don't report to him. As the best engineer on the project, he teaches and manages by continually asking, "Why?" He reviews the new vehicle's status not by reading reports, not by checking off completed tasks against a milestone list, but by looking at the prototypes and analyses himself.

The team is cross-functional. At Toyota, that might mean one member who knows engines, another computers and electrical systems, another ergonomics, another styling, another manufacturing (which is important, because once you've designed the car, truck or SUV, you need to be able to build it in a factory) and another sales or marketing (to make sure that what you design and build is something that customers want to buy). To at least some extent, team members can help out or fill in for each other.

In a Lean Agency, teams are also cross-functional, comprising members from creative (copy and art direction), media planning, maybe production, public relations (Even if the account doesn't have a PR component at the agency, wouldn't it be nice to have some good ideas consistent with the advertising? Or advertising ideas with PR potential?) and either marketing, account planning or account service—an agency in micro-

Brand Advertising

cosm, minus the support and drudge work like accounting, media buying, human resources, etc. Traffic wouldn't show up at all, either on the team or in the Lean Agency as a whole, for reasons which we'll explain shortly. And the team will have a leader. It doesn't matter from which function, so long as the leader really knows his or her stuff.

In the Lean Agency, this cross-functionality is not a matter of democracy or functional equal opportunity—it's a matter of necessity. An advertising agency's product is ideas, and the traditional Fat Agency structure tends to limit who's allowed to have them. The Doyle Dane Bernbach revolution confined generating ideas to the creative team because, before the 1960s, too many scientific advertisers, account managers who valued easy approvals over truly effective work, and other incompetents were able to not only suggest, but dictate ideas—usually trite ones. But the same system that filtered out bad ideas from mid-20th Century hacks also works to filter out good ideas from savvy, conscientious 21st Century professionals who just don't happen to be official creatives. And it shouldn't, because no one has a monopoly on good ideas:

- A print producer was the first to think of scratch-and-sniff fragrance ads in magazines.
- A media planner was probably the one who thought of "bookend" 15-second spots, which creative teams then began creating as two-part stories which deterred zapping by building suspense from the unresolved ending of bookend one to the resolution in bookend two.
- One of the most ingenious hospital campaigns of the early 1990s came about because a media planner figured out a way to buy L-shaped fractional-page news paper ads, conforming to the shape of the main visual, which was a foot or an arm in a cast.

In a campaign a computer hardware manufacturer client was targeting to home automation (smart-home) decision-makers at Microsoft, our media partner, Tony Booth, came up with a way to cost-effectively use television as a highly targeted, selective medium. (It involved cable systems serving bedroom communities in and around Redmond, Washington, and ended up with a $10 million sale to Microsoft—almost 100 times the client's total media, production and creative-fee investment.)

The famous "Got Milk?" campaign resulted from an account planner's diagnostic research and his insights about what it really showed.

Brand Advertising

After routine research established what people liked to drink milk with, the account planner conducted an inspired experiment. He got respondents to avoid drinking milk with those foods for a week, and noted how grumpy it made them. The rest was history.

Unlike the Toyota system, the Lean Agency team should also at critical times include the customer (i.e., client decision-makers) for reasons we'll discuss in the next chapter.

FAT AGENCY	**LEAN AGENCY**
Administrative Based Totally concerned with budgets, schedules, rules, resources, adminstrative issues	**Work Based** Totally concerned with craft issues: decision-making, customer interface, leadership
Interfaced One-on-one communication as needed, otherwise through memos and formal channels	**Interactive** Totally open teaming as people resolve issues, perceive need; spontaneous, informal
Information Guarded Keep info to yourself, ration to others only when really needed	**Concurrent Information** Available and easily accessible to all as a way of life
Low Proficiency Compliance valued over ability. Peter Principle creates worker brain drain.	**High Proficiency** Ability and experience rewarded. Team members learn from exercising responsibility.
Ad-hoc cross-functionality Informal, only when necessary	**Ingrained cross-functionality** Systematic and highly effective

One thing this cross-functional team is not is something that Y&R instituted during the first time Bruce Goldman worked there. It was called the Product Group, consisted of everyone in the New York Office assigned to a specific account (often more than 30 people) and seemed to exist solely for the purpose of giving everyone huge amounts of time to score points by taking public potshots at their fellow group members' work.

Brand Advertising

Like Toyota teams, Lean Agency teams are empowered. Empowered to make the decisions and call the shots free from professional second-guessers in ivory towers. Of course, the leader's the one who really makes decisions, but the leader leads instead of bossing. The leader motivates, questions, coaches, trains and facilitates the work of everyone adding value, rather than telling them what to do and how to do it. This way of doing business gives believers in top-down hierarchies the creeps —not because it works badly, but because of the very ways in which it works so well.

One way it works too well for comfort is that it encourages a continuous flow of the work, first to the client and then to the media and the target audience, adding value every step of the way. Because this process ferrets out and eliminates any activity that fails to add value, the only people needed are those who actually touch the product (in this case the advertising) and keep it moving. And since these people are all responsible for themselves and the value of their own output, there go whole layers of supervisors, managers, directors, department heads, and lower-level nonessential personnel.

Our research shows that when a business goes Lean, it cuts labor costs about 40 percent, and that's just for starters. One client we worked with had five layers of management between general manager and shop floor worker. The plant employed about 400 workers, not a particularly large number. But reporting to the general manager on the manufacturing side was a head of operations, followed by the head of production, the head of the shop, a layer of supervisors, and a cadre of group leaders. (Each group leader was responsible for a cell of shop floor workers.) This was in contrast to one of the most efficient and productive companies we've worked with that employed more than 1,000 workers but had only two management levels. Eventually, the first client's plant was changed to look like the second client's.

Because the Lean Agency is less hierarchical, there's less bureaucracy to impede teams and drag out decision-making. Traditional hierarchies usually are not only cumbersome and slow to act, they're costly—and the biggest cost is often that of lost opportunity. The Lean Agency pushes decision-making to those people closest to a situation. Who can possibly be in a better position to recognize what needs to be done than the people right there on the spot? So going Lean saves even more than labor costs;

it cuts decision-making time and saddles the company with fewer bad decisions.

The typical administrative-based approach you find at a Fat Agency reviews projects and makes decisions by counting how many tasks were completed by when, kind of like counting the trees instead of seeing the forest. The forest—the content and quality of the work itself—is usually evaluated externally by the client or internally by some kind of default.

So instead of making hard decisions, the Fat Agency backs into them as deadlines approach; the tighter the deadline, the better it looks. In the Lean Agency, on the other hand, smart team leaders who understand all the issues make timely decisions and lead through coaching.

Lean organizations create deliberate uncertainty and chaos and move towards eventual order. But in Fat organizations, as reality fails to follow systems, the work moves from deliberate order to eventual chaos as the managers wonder what's the latest eventuality that their systems failed to cover.

Their problem is never that the controls and systems don't work, of course; it's just that they're not fully followed. The problem is never a bankrupt philosophy; it's one of insufficient compliance with the bankrupt philosophy in question. Remember what true believers from the American left were saying about the Soviet Union until the the Berlin Wall fell? The real problem with Communism wasn't that there was something inherently wrong with it, just that nobody had ever tried it in its pure, unadulterated, complete form. Try telling that to Mikhail Gorbachev.

In the Lean Agency, decision-making is divided between the team's leader and its members. This doesn't mean that decisions are made by consensus; that's the recipe for delay and bland, lowest-common-denominator mediocrity.

Rather, the team leader makes the key decisions about the product, while the team members make decisions about the process. These can cover anything from who'll fill in for an art director who's out sick to whether to work late to how to improve the process itself.

When the team leader assigns someone to a job, the team as a whole exerts subtle but noticeable peer pressure to make sure he or she does it on time and well. When there's a problem, the team decides how to fix it; and having made that decision, the team will either make it work or quickly find another way that does.

The team as a whole evaluates its members' individual performance, so you know where their loyalties will lie.

The team leader sets target times for the key steps where things have to come together and establishes exactly what will have to be ready at each of these times. Everyone understands and never, ever, misses these dates. The leader also spells out exactly who's responsible for which results.

And then the team goes to work, taking responsibility for setting their own schedules for meeting the dates, sharing information with everyone who needs it. The leader will coordinate and consolidate the work but not micromanage it, because we're dealing with responsible grownups here. And those responsible grownups will do what engineers call "heavy prototyping" (i.e., lots of strategies, creative concepts, alternative media plans, etc.) along the way, so that decisions can be made on the basis of something tangible, and so that everyone can learn something, react to it, and build on it.

This is a reactional process, and the Lean Agency recognizes it as such. Fat Agencies, on the other hand, treat it as a transactional one. They build in all kinds of systems, measurements and reports which give them delusions of adequacy. This illusion of control fools them into thinking their work is much better than it really is.

Within the team, everyone's comments are equal and welcome. Freethinking is encouraged. But it's not the U. S. Senate. Majority rule doesn't matter, consensus doesn't count, and filibustering will not be tolerated. The team leader has overall responsibility and makes all final decisions—including when to end discussion and move on.

Individuals are expected to fight for what they perceive as best. They're also expected to know the difference between that kind of fighting and petty turf battles.

Someone who's fully bought into the Lean Agency concept has bought into a mindset that compels the continual pursuit of excellence in order to advance the *organization's* mission. Team members all know that a particular job which needs to be done today or next week simply contributes to the greater whole, the bigger task of what the firm is about, which is to be the best.

On assembly lines in Lean Production factories, teams of blue-collar, hourly-wage workers are trusted and empowered to make key decisions. When they spot a problem, they decide how to fix it—no need to call in management. If they see a quality defect problem in an assembly operation, for example, they're not only allowed but obliged to shut down the line until the problem is fixed. (In a Fat Production company, this would be unthinkable; only the general manager has the authority to permit such an action.)

Why shouldn't well-educated, high-salary professionals creating value for customers in a service business such as an advertising agency enjoy the same trust and empowerment?

Teams are "empowered" because they can decide on the best course of action, then take it. Members must shift from a mindset where supervisors tell them what to do to one where group members take initiative and the group as a whole makes decisions. They'll have to think outside the box in order to determine how processes can be improved and what changes should be implemented. Perhaps as important, teams can help build an atmosphere of cooperation and *esprit de corps*. Provided, of course, that its people learn how to work as team players.

Teamwork can result in an extraordinary experience that members will never forget. The bonding that results can be very strong indeed. Even in groups with modest missions, teamwork can replace apathy and discouragement with pride and enthusiasm. At the very least, team members will have learned to listen sincerely and speak the truth instead of just venting and bellyaching.

Caring about the team's success and about teammates is half the battle. It can go a long way in helping people learn how to put what may be good for the group as a whole ahead of selfish motives. Every effort should be made to keep membership consistent from one day to the next. Individuals should remain together as much as possible so that *esprit de corps* can build.

A team can be almost any group with closely linked jobs and should cut across what would be different departments in a Fat Agency. To break down the barriers, we think of team members as representatives of various disciplines rather than as having different functions. The distinction is subtle, but it helps take a wrecking ball to those departmental walls. Having people from different organizations—such as clients—participating in a project is also important; they can often see things that people with day-to-day involvement may be too close to notice.

Workers on a Lean Producer's factory floor are physically grouped into teams of production cells. Within the large ad agency, the same concept can apply. Each "cell," or team, will be responsible for all of the work on one or more advertising accounts. They'll meet regularly to discuss and solve problems. It's also important for team leaders to live there, too, so that they're clearly part of the team—not part of some faraway, elitist, ivory-tower management group.

Empowered teams are a fundamental way of working throughout the Lean Agency. In a figurative sense, they help bring down interdepartmental walls, but we've found that it can actually help if the owners literally bring walls down as well. This creates as much transparency as possible by putting everyone together where being able to see one another encourages interaction. Back when Scali McCabe Sloves had two accounts and more owners than employees, Sam Scali and Ed McCabe shared a large office and did great work. Together.

It also works for bigger groups of people. On the ground floor of the Honda Motors research and development center's office building in Togichi, Japan, "200 or more workers sit at desks in a single immense and undivided room, 100 percent cubicle-free."[13]

In your organization you, too, might consider placing all your team members' offices or cubicles next to each other, maybe grouped around a small conference area.

Rather than segregating them into departments by job function as they probably are now, group them by team. Whether the team head is someone from account service, media, creative or even PR shouldn't matter. Pick the best, brightest, most knowledgeable leader. Each group might be considered, and consider themselves, a small agency. A six-person shop striving to make a name for itself is likely to turn out more and better work than six people spread out on different floors in different departments who communicate only occasionally by memo, telephone or e-mail. To encourage interaction and togetherness, consider having offices with clear glass walls, or, as we've done in our agency, no walls at all. With that kind of setup, interaction has to take place, and leaders can't help but be available and attentive.

In the Lean Agency, leaders exist to serve. To motivate and coach. To facilitate the work of others. Moving a desk or office often helps supervisors make the mental switch to this role, but not always, because becoming a Lean Agency means being able to live with a paradox. Top managers and team leaders must be simultaneously directive and empowering, and these qualities don't exactly go hand in hand.

In terms of the final product decisions, in terms of the overall Lean direction of the agency, leadership has to be strong, unambiguous and clear about the path. At the same time, leaders must continually empower their teams along the way, giving them complete authority to carry out their assigned tasks as the members, individually and collectively, see fit.

It's not easy, because throughout their careers successful managers have been the ones who came up with the good ideas and pushed them through. (That's why the Peter Principle made them managers.) They aren't used to or comfortable with others having them; in fact, they may see the very justification for their corporate existence threatened. They may feel that successes their team members achieve reflect poorly on them personally.

Unless they're much bigger than most people, they'll at the very least feel anxious about the change to empowered teams and fearful that their authority has been undermined. They may even become angry or, perhaps, genuinely and openly skeptical. Either way, they'll say this new arrangement's successes are temporary flukes. And they'll make it a self-fulfilling prophecy so long as they're allowed to dig Lean Production's grave with their mouths.

That's why the Lean Agency must be impatient from top to bottom. Impatient with doubt and delay. Impatient with foot-dragging. Impatient with empty theorizing that obstructs delivering tangible results. Impatient with heel-dragging reactionaries taking too long to get on board. In its most productive form, impatience should translate into a fire lit under the organization to realize the vision.

But impatience, while needed and potentially constructive, should be tempered with a healthy dose of realism, particularly about how fast to move ahead and how fast the agency's size and number of accounts will let it keep up.

The balance of impatience and realism also shapes the Lean Agency's

Brand Advertising

critical element of setting goals—goals for waste reduction, lead-time reduction and other quality improvements. Surprisingly, management's goals will often turn out to be on the conservative side; empowered teams often set more aggressive goals than management will—and usually achieve them.

This raises a critical issue concerning management style. Positive reinforcement is important, and this means celebrating successes. But it's just as important to *not* punish a team for failing to achieve an aggressive goal. Rather, management should act as coach to help the team understand what went wrong (including assessing whether the goal was too aggressive) and to help the team learn from the experience. This type of mutual support goes a long way toward building top performers.

Even after the changeover, some leaders continue to boss rather than lead. So what's an agency president or marketing director to do?

Two things – a carrot and a stick. The stick is making it clear that the leader has a choice of either leading or leaving. The carrot is a "job well done." Improving performance and accomplishing goals provide more motivating rewards than the feeling of power over others. This will work if the focus can be shifted where it belongs, to end results—to filling customer needs, to increased quality, to lower costs.

Team play, decision-making down the line, and putting the customer first, for example, are what make Toyota the envy of their industries. Team play is what the Lean Agency is all about, and everyone's thinking will need to change to realize it.

Managers will have to learn to let go, to become coaches instead of being in a position to give orders. Workers will have to learn to take responsibility—and the risks that go with it. (Toyota assembly workers have to be willing to stop a line if quality's threatened; so does a Lean Agency team member if the campaign under development is starting to go off the rails.)

Everyone will have to learn to work together, to replace an authoritarian climate with a participative one. And to understand, not just intellectually but emotionally, that what's good for the whole must take precedence over what may be viewed as good for an individual. They'll have to learn to work in a way that puts all these fine-sounding theoretical ideas into daily, living practice.

Brand Advertising

This requires that a process be in place which forces the reality. Maybe this process includes daily "how can we improve?" meetings. Maybe it means establishing a mechanism for suggestions and a deadline for responding to them. Maybe it means finding and institutionalizing ways to facilitate the free flow of ideas. And maybe it means all of the above.

Typically, Lean Agency teams have 10-15 minute meetings at the start of each day. They look at yesterday's performance and today's goals. They review work assignments and adjust for any special situations. If someone on the team is away on a shoot, or if someone has to leave early, they'll discuss it and decide how to handle it. They'll discuss where the group stands; is it ahead or behind in terms of meeting deadlines? If it's behind, they'll decide what to do to catch up. Teams also meet for a half-hour, once a week, to discuss performance issues.

Add up the time spent in meetings, and you'll find that workers spend an hour and three quarters each week—less than some Fat Agencies spend just reading their unexpurgated status report aloud to the assembled troops every Monday morning.

But sometimes, teams will need to meet longer, particularly to discuss an area that Fat Agencies either neglect or fail to take seriously—suggestions on how to improve.

A Lean Agency will review, approve and adopt improvement ideas as far down in the organization as possible, usually at the Team level. This means that team leaders must have authority to approve improvement expenditures up to a certain cost—or, if they already have that authority, perhaps a higher cost. (Maybe that'll emotionally compensate leaders bruised from having lost their bossing authority.)

Sometimes suggestions include things the team can't put in place without help from another functional area. Or sometimes they're for improving work outside the team's area. Either way, the Lean Agency must have a bias for evaluating and adopting suggestions quickly, rejecting them only for good reason, and communicating either the adoption status or rejection reasons back to the person who first made the suggestion. That's what Toyota does, and their management says they implement about 90 percent of all suggestions and give constant feedback on where implementation stands.

Teams may also need extra meeting time to deal with unforeseen problems. Maybe one's arisen doing the work for a specific client. Team members can set up a talk with the client to understand firsthand what's at issue and discuss how the problem can be solved. When a staffer comes back from such a visit, the rest of the team listens carefully, because it's like hearing from a comrade-in-arms just back from the front. Armed with the front-line scouting report, the team members put on their thinking caps and attack the problem in a better way.

A crucial element of successful team work is information-sharing. It's ironic that marketing and advertising are information-based businesses—whose managers traditionally guard information, even keep it under lock and key. After all, information is power. In a Fat Agency, it's the power to hinder. In the Lean Agency, it's the power to excel.

If employees don't know how the agency or marketing department is doing, if they don't even know how they themselves are doing, how can they be expected to do better?

This is one reason that Lean Agency management makes sure everyone knows what's going on. But not the only reason. You'll recall that a sense of belonging, an *esprit de corps,* is part of what enables an organization to get ahead and stay ahead of the competition. It's pretty difficult to be proud of what you are and how you're doing if you know neither.

Readily available information, information that can be had for the asking, is not all we're talking about here. We mean making sure people know what's happening, day by day. Not just at daily meetings, but the whole working day long. Not only on visible charts, but in conversation. In short, information in the Lean Agency is in the open for all to see and use, not buried in a password-protected computer or locked in a manager's desk.

Communication in advertising has gotten considerably more visual since the 1960s. So should communication within the Lean Agency.

Visual management—usually in the form of scoreboards positioned where everyone on the team can see them—tracks performance and gives workers feedback on how they're doing; management is by sight, not by memo, status report or computer. In factories, performance is posted hourly in a column next to pre-established goals. The reasons for variances, plus or minus, are accounted for in a column reserved for "remarks." This way, a team can see where it stands in relation to its output goal for the shift and adjust its work accordingly. They can also identify obstacles that may be standing in the way of their objectives. Scoreboards, by the way, are only one example of how a Lean Producer brings information from the domain of a privileged few out into the open. Instead of being hoarded, information is made to flow throughout the organization, empowering team members to take actions that will improve performance.

Why not try it in an ad agency or marketing department? It will eliminate the need for a traffic department, because everyone will be able to see just how a project is coming, or not coming, along. And if it's not, team pressure may then be brought to bear to get those "little" jobs done that might otherwise be swept under the rug and hold up the big things.

Lean Producers adhere to the principle that quality should be built in, not inspected in. This means making marketing communications people responsible for their own work.

If it's a proofreader's job to make sure spelling and grammar are correct, that takes the heat off the copywriter and encourages sloppiness. True, you need a second set of eyes to see what's actually set in type (instead of what the writer's eyes expect to see), but any reasonably literate team member can do that.

If art directors don't have to worry whether what they output conforms to publications' mechanical specs, one of two things will happen. Either a person will have to be added to the payroll to resize or rescale InDesign or other computer files, or an outside service bureau will have to be paid to do it.

Either way, the work's going to take longer and cost more to do, with no value added. It may even subtract value, because when someone other than the originator does the work, that's begging for mistakes (through lack of firsthand knowledge) to creep in. Some things, like expert-level Photoshop retouching, you have to send out, but a correctly sized mechanical shouldn't be one of them.

It may be a bit scary at first to make people responsible for their own output. Especially those who have relied on others to sweep up after them all their careers.

But consider the experience of manufacturing companies that have gone Lean. Assembly-line workers are responsible for what they turn out. If they can be, so should skilled copywriters, art directors, media planners and account managers. The key is to place all the responsibility squarely on their shoulders—no safety nets—so they have to take it seriously.

We mentioned earlier that Toyota employs no quality inspectors. Their plant in Kentucky has about ten slots at the end of the line for cars that need rework. Thousands of vehicles are turned out every day. Yet, if those ten slots ever become filled, the production line is stopped so the problem, whatever it was, can be found and corrected.

Fat Production automakers, in contrast, have much larger rework areas, accommodating hundreds of cars and routinely full to the brim. Yet management doesn't wonder what's wrong. Rework is expected and accepted. These mass producers often proudly point to the large number of "quality inspectors" in white coats on their payrolls. Their inspectors actually are engaged in correcting what could and should have been done right in the first place.

Now, for "quality inspectors in white coats" think "levels of agency management," and for "rework" think "revisions." Then ask yourself why the same principle of identifying who owns responsibility couldn't work in an advertising agency or your own marketing communications department.

The Lean Agency's very basis is the relentless pursuit of perfection. This characteristic is what makes all the others possible. Nobody's ever satisfied with progress. No matter how far everybody's come, they don't rest on laurels. The culture ensures, even demands, a continual and constant search for better ways to do even the smallest tasks. Looking for ways to cut waste, looking for ways to improve quality, looking for ways to cut inventory, looking for ways to do things better, quicker, faster, easier, becomes ingrained.

And as the search goes on, it's important to celebrate successes.

Most managers are, correctly, quick to have a meeting about what's going wrong. But for positive reinforcement, meetings also should be held about what's going right.

There should also be celebrations. The head of an account group or the director of marketing might buy coffee for a team that's scored a success. Or maybe a cake complete with candles. Or pizza. Everyone who had a hand in the success should be invited, but only those who did. Letting interlopers join in destroys the celebration's meaning and waters down its significance. When others score their own successes, they'll get their own free pizza and attaboy.

Success, like obstruction, is a self-fulfilling prophecy. When everyone from management to mailroom keeps pursuit of perfection foremost in their minds, when this pursuit becomes a never-ending process—though even the leanest of companies can approach perfection only asymptotically—then slow, complacent, Fat Agencies become fast, nimble, Lean Agencies. With many more successes to celebrate.

Chapter Five
Leading sacred cows to slaughter.

We've been discussing Fat Agency features that waste time, but there are others that add cost but not value by making the work flow stop flowing. In the Lean Agency, that's only one of the kinds of waste that's fair game. The more waste of any and all kinds you eliminate, the closer you come to the improvement you're striving for. *Muda* is the Japanese word for "waste," and in the Lean Agency it's practically a swear word. It's not the client, or the suppliers, or the team leaders, or the other teams, or the people you don't like on your own team who are the enemy. It's *muda*, and like the army and air force in Japanese monster movies, everyone in a Lean Agency mobilizes to destroy it. Because *muda* is what keeps agency people from creating value for customers or clients. *Muda* is what distracts them from seeing their work from the customer or client's point of view. *Muda* is the enemy of marketing communications that, first and foremost, sell product. That break out and shine above the din of competing communications. That project the desired image and make consumers like the brand. *Muda* delays, diverts and deters the agency from delivering all this at the lowest possible cost and with no problems or surprises.

It's a wily adversary, a master of camouflage and concealment. *Muda* can hide itself in the way agencies open jobs, how they create and present concepts, how they produce the finished work and get it out to the media. And what makes *muda* so hard to root out and kill is its uncanny ability to disguise itself as some of a Fat Agency's most established, least questioned practices.

When you get right down to it, hunting down and killing *muda* means open season on sacred cows. By sacred cows we mean dumb ways of doing things that everyone follows because that's how it's always been done.

Here's an example. In 1940, after Britain had left far too many of its soldiers on the Dunkirk beaches, a Royal Army commission started looking for ways to make the most combat use of the forces they still had. One day, commission members visited a motorized artillery battery and observed four-man gun crews in action. One man loaded shells in the cannon's breech. A second man worked the breech lever to close the breech on the new round and eject the spent casings. A third man aimed and fired the cannon. And a fourth man just stood there. The commission members wondered why, so they went back to headquarters and checked the records. They checked the World War I records, they checked the Boer War records, they checked the Crimean War records, and only when they got to the Napoleonic Wars (ended in 1815) records did they find the answer—the fourth man's job was to hold the reins of the horses.

Fat agencies have their sacred cows, too. One is their tendency, like the inflexible Fat Producers of the 1950s, to gear for peak demand. This wastes talent and money, particularly the client's money, as the old

$$\text{Cost} + \text{Profit Margin (i.e., commissions and fees)} = \text{Price}$$

formula kicks in. Movie studios illustrate the difference between how Fat Agencies staff for peak demand and Lean Agencies staff for customer pull. From the 1920s through the 1950s, big Hollywood movie studios had huge numbers of people as permanent staff: contract actors, contract directors, contract screenwriters and film editors, contract composers and film crews. They owned huge back lots with all kinds of standing sets. And since they were constantly turning out movies the way Boeing's World War II factory was turning out B-17s, this made economic sense. But then, once television started cutting into movie viewership (and hence the number of movies made each year) and smaller, independent studios started increasing movie competition, having those huge masses of employees under full-time contract stopped making sense. Eventually, the big studios realized this, killed their sacred cow and reorganized to survive. Today, each has a cadre of key decision-makers. Actors, directors, screenwriters, editors, set designers, gaffers, grips, directors of photography, best boys and the lot are all freelancers signed for a particular feature. You may and often do find the same freelancers working for the same studios feature after feature after feature, but the studios hire them for work, as opposed to jobs.

Advertising agencies can learn from their example. Instead of overstaffing to meet occasional peak demand, they can staff with key people and teams for default demand, then add talented freelancers for peaks.

Using the in-house team members as a cadre of leaders for expansion teams of talented freelancers helps the agency get temporarily bigger without getting fatter.

Another sacred cow is in-house big, expensive, capital-intensive equipment. Once upon a time, having this kind of stuff around made sense. Back in the pre-videotape days, when the only way to view mixed final cuts of television commercials was in 16- or 35-millimeter interlock, it made sense for agencies that did a lot of broadcast work to own, at the very least, a Moviola. Today, you can review MP4 files on your computer or smartphone; and the free iMovie 10.1.1 will let you edit them. In 1960s Los Angeles, when it took three days for agencies to get photostats (one day for the stat house courier to wend his way through the Southern California sprawl for the pickup, one day to make the stats, one day for the courier to wend his way back with the delivery), in-house photostat machines made sense. Today, with sizing by computer file and delivery by e-mail, they don't.

One more sacred cow is the knee-jerk assumption that effective advertising requires huge budgets for original film, photography and music, plus special effects. It needn't. In fact, an overabundance of resources can often make the work less, rather than more, effective.

In 1957, Professor C. Northcote Parkinson first articulated the law that bears his name—"Work expands so as to fill the time available for its completion."

In examining British Admiralty records, he found that in the 1920s, when the United Kingdom was busy dismantling and disarming the Royal Navy, the Admiralty had more and more civilian bureaucrats on payroll—more, in fact, than they'd had to administer the world's largest naval fleet just a decade before in World War I. In the late 1940s, he found, as the UK was giving its colonies their freedom left and right, the British Colonial Office was employing more and more bureaucrats to administer fewer and fewer colonies.[14]

Parkinson's Law applies just as much to physical resources as time. In the 1960s and '70s, Dr. Edward de Bono was conducting research with children who were still too young to have their minds conventionalized. In one experiment, a child would be escorted to the threshold of a doorway. On the floor would be two boards and two pieces of string. The child would be told that the object of the experiment was to cross the room to another doorway on the far side without his or her feet touching the floor. So the child would look at the room, look down at the boards and strings, think a bit and then, as the light bulb went off, tie one board to each foot, and walk across the room, with de Bono timing the whole thing. Then de Bono would repeat the experiment with another group of children, and only one board and string. Same thing, except that this time, the children would tie the board to one foot and hop across the room—in about half the time. De Bono pointed out that any of the kids from the two-board group could have used the one-board solution, but even at their young age, they'd absorbed the societal conditioning which says that when you're given a problem to solve and resources for solving it, you're supposed to use up all the resources.

Another resource to which Parkinson's Law applies is money. From 1979 to 1990, The Public Purpose (www.publicpurpose.com) reported, the very government subsidies allocated to lower the per-vehicle-mile operating costs of "166 public transit agencies accounting for more than 93 percent of transit operating costs (motor bus, electric bus, light rail and heavy rail)" actually raised them. The agencies with the biggest subsidies saw the biggest operating cost increases, while those with the least did best at holding the line—some to 0 percent increase. During the same eleven-year span, "the private bus industry, which uses the same factors of production and operates in the same labor market as public transit, costs per mile *declined more than 10 percent* [our emphasis]. "

In advertising, Fat Agencies used up all the available resources and then some. In the late 1960s, Benton & Bowles, for example, produced a Contac cold medicine commercial that could have been lifted from "Gold Diggers of 1933" or any other Hollywood musical choreographed by Busby Berkeley. They bought the rights to the song, "Take Good Care of Yourself (You Belong to Me)," rescored and rerecorded it, and had on-camera chorus girls singing it while tap-dancing in formation. Stan Freberg created an even bigger extravaganza—with Hollywood and Broadway actress Ann Miller, no less—for Campbell's Great American Soups. At least Freberg had the grace to make the actor playing her husband's last line, "Great. But do you have to make such a production out of it?" Gee, all that expensive buildup for that one-liner (get it?).

Brand Advertising

The industry has learned too much to do that anymore. Instead, they use the latest computer-generated imagery and feature-movie-like special effects as a subsititue for ideas.

One example that comes to mind is a Hal Riney commercial comparing First Union Securities to a mountain. It created a surreally mountainous structure of 1930s skyscrapers, flying cars, clouds and other scary effects, just to build up to a weak one-liner: "So come to the mountain. Or, if you prefer, the mountain will come to you."

Either way, the hope is that a lot of money spent on razzle-dazzle will not only add to the Fat Agency commission or production markup, but will also mask the total absence of any idea.

It doesn't have to be that way, and in the late 1970s, in Minneapolis of all places, a copywriter named Tom McElligott started proving it. McElligott was to go on to become the creative force behind Fallon McElligott, which, with The Martin Agency (Steve's old place), was arguably the Doyle Dane Bernbach of the 1980s and '90s.

Back in the '70s, McElligott had a full-time job at Bozell and a freelance business called Lunch Hour Ltd. The latter had small clients with commensurately small budgets. So McElligott developed an unorthodox technique. His ads used not original photography, but substantially cheaper stock photos, which his headlines put in a whole new context. For a local hair stylist shop's campaign, he used images of the Three Stooges, Richard Nixon and Albert Einstein (see below) with the headline, "A bad haircut can make anyone look dumb." For a public service campaign for the Episcopal Church, he coupled a stock illustration of a greeting-card Santa Claus with the headline, "Whose birthday is it anyway?"

Today, with so much high-resolution royalty-free photography downloadable from the Internet, the technique of using imagination to put stock images in refreshing new contexts is even Leaner.

Brand Advertising

A Lean technique: headlines that customize stock photos.

Brand Advertising

**The photo is stock. The concept isn't.
Imaginative use of royalty-free images makes advertising Leaner.**

Another sacred cow in print advertising, in that it's something the industry's done so long that people forget why, is defaulting to four-color ads. Back in the 1930s, when most ads were black and white, the Y&R-commissioned Gallup research showed that four-color magazine ads attracted more readership. Pick up any consumer magazine today, and you'll find that just about every full-page or larger ad is in color. As a result, four-color production per se no longer makes an ad stand out. In television, where there's no extra charge for color production, some agencies have helped spots stand out (while conveying the feel of a serious message) by producing in black and white. In print, where magazines charge a premium for four-color, clients can spends tens of thousands of dollars extra for the dubious privilege of making their ads blend into the editorial and advertising environment. (For example, at the one-time rate, a one-page, black and white, national insertion in *People* magazine costs $250,100. In color, it's $357,200. That's $107,100—or almost 43 percent—more.)

Brand Advertising

In broadcast as well as print, it's proven over and over again that less is more. Take away the golden crutches of spectacular but irrelevant production techniques, and you're forced to come up with ideas that can not only stand, but walk, run and pole vault on their own two legs. Tom Monahan, co-founder of Leonard/Monahan in Providence, now travels the country coaching global corporations on creativity and giving speeches to ad groups. One of his speeches features a cassette of arresting, involving, intrusive, effective really low-budget (less than $5,000) television commercials where the special effects are the truly compelling ideas. In early 1998, we were faced with a similar challenge on behalf of a local florist. They'd done a barter deal with one Richmond television station for $1,000 worth of air time, which Tony Booth decided to put into one day's worth of 15-second spots the day before Valentine's Day. That year, the day before Valentine's, February 13, just happened to fall on a Friday, which inspired the commercial on page 80.

The images cost a total of $40. The whole spot, from blank piece of paper through master and air dubs, came in at $1,813. In just one day's airing, it increased the client's Valentine's Day business 85 percent over the previous year.

Like the kids with two boards in de Bono's experiments, anyone in an agency with a big-budget project could butcher this sacred cow and do more with less, but somehow they never manage to.

A sacred cow that the 1960s Creative Revolution killed but which the computer has, ironically, resurrected is tight comps (comprehensive layouts), with headlines and often body copy set in actual type and actual (or close to actual) photography and/or illustrations. These are time-consuming and therefore costly to make, because you're in effect fully producing an ad when it's still only a concept. Up through the 1950s, this was the standard form for presenting ads to clients—because the clients were presumably either too stupid to be able to visualize the finish, so gullible that they'd be so impressed by a high level of finish that they'd miss the low-level, mediocre concept, or so insecure that they needed all this fancy preproduction as proof that they were getting their money's worth.

In the 1960s, Doyle Dane Bernbach started presenting ads to clients as marker roughs or tissue roughs—so called because the art director roughed in the visuals and hand-lettered the headlines with a marker pen

MUSIC: CHOPIN'S "DEAD MARCH" FROM SAUL, UNDER
FVO: If you think today's

FVO: ... try forgetting what tomorrow is.

The Foliage Place
Same Day Delivery
747-5994

MUSIC: CONTINUES TO END OF SPOT

on cheap, tissue-like tracing paper. The images were squiggles, the font was Handwriting Medium, and the body copy was a bunch of roughly parallel lines. But you know what? The clients got it. So marker roughs became the standard form of presentation—until computers started to make their way into art departments in the late 1980s. Agencies started churning out their roughs by computer because it was faster. They could even churn out finished comps faster, and therein lay the problem. Once you find you can do something, human nature dictates that sooner or later you will. The desktop computer was initially touted as the harbinger of the paperless office. Hah! As soon as people with desktops and database software discovered they could start generating more different kinds of reports, they promptly started generating more different kinds of reports.

Brand Advertising

On paper. With multiple copies for distribution. (This was an early manifestation of Parkinson's Law of Data, which says, "Data expands to fill the space available for storage.")

Increasingly widespread use of time-saving computers created lots of time-wasting unforeseen consequences of this nature.

For example, the United States Defense Department went to PowerPoint presentations on laptop computers as the medium for military briefings. This was quicker and cheaper than the old way of preparing briefings on slides and overhead-projector cells. Quicker and cheaper in theory, that is. In practice, ambitious briefing officers out to win promotion by impressing their superiors started investing inordinate amounts of time picking razzle-dazzle fonts and devising cool screen layouts—more time and attention, ultimately, then they spent on their briefings' contents. To save all that wasted time, money and misdirected effort, the Pentagon had to order that fonts and screen layouts be restricted to an authorized few .

It's no wonder, then, that when Fat Agencies started saving time by going to computer roughs—typing in the headlines in actual fonts, scanning in reference photographs and setting dummy type (or even actual body copy), again in real type faces—the same kind of thing happened. Because the resulting roughs looked so literal and finished, art directors couldn't leave them be. They started designing them. This accomplished four things: (1) It made certain kinds of art directors—the kinds who have to waste 15 minutes fine-tuning the color bars on the monitor before they'll allow an *audio* mix to start—feel better, (2) it reintroduced client quibbles over "I don't like the way that woman looks" or "I really hate that type face," which diverted attention from the basic concept's merits (or lack thereof), (3) lavishing computerized preproduction on concepts the agency had fallen in love with gave them a tool for pressuring clients into buying them, and (4) it got the meter running again, big-time.

Some agencies, like Young & Rubicam (We're not trying to single out Y&R here; it's just that we know about them from firsthand experience.) maintained in-house photography, and later video, studios for the sole purpose of making things look professionally finished for the client—and for testing completed ad ideas, which brings us to another sacred cow.

Research can be either a major source of insights for a Lean Agency or a major cause of *muda* for a Fat Agency. It all depends on how and why you use it.

Used diagnostically, to learn something important from the target audience before the first concept is ever thought of, it's a treasure. When conducting a focus group about women's clothing, an astute moderator noticed that whenever the topic of bra sizes came up, the smaller-breasted women in the focus group would go into classic defense posture, crossing their arms over their chests. This observation led to the idea of the Anne Klein A-Line clothing brand exclusively for petite women. Talk about creating value!

But used to second-guess completed work, research is major *muda*. Recruiting enough focus groups representative of target audiences in enough cities, then renting properly equipped facilities (with two-way mirrors, video cameras, conference tables, etc.) is *muda*. Producing special materials for presentation to the focus groups is more *muda*. Flying a moderator and agency staff all around the country just to sit through all the groups and later review the videotapes and a report is Son of *Muda*. Having your representative consumers turn, like werewolves, from normal human beings into dreaded Critics of Advertising, as invariably happens in focus groups about halfway through the session, is I Was a Teenage *Muda* for the FBI. And then going back and changing the work to conform to these at best questionable findings so you can repeat the process (again and again) is Lord of the *Muda*.

But that's nothing compared to testing television concepts. Because there, you're spending thousands of dollars for either crude animations or edited video images, mixed to original audio tracks, which will be shown to consumers under, shall we say, somewhat artificial conditions: at shopping-mall intercepts, or in theater-like studios where respondents have to twist a dial either clockwise or counterclockwise to show their interest or disinterest in what they're watching (at tens of thousands of dollars per test). Just like kicking back in front of the tube at home, right? And of course you're testing two or three such concepts against each other, so the testing company will invariably recommend that you build a commercial the way Dr. Frankenstein built men, by putting the allegedly high-viewer-interest parts of one commercial together with the allegedly high-viewer-interest parts of the others, then testing the monster which results. You could run a decent broadcast schedule on what Fat Agencies end up making you pay for the test/revise/ test/revise, etc., cycle. Provided you have any left to produce the final spot and buy the air time. And you may not, after you get through paying through the nose for the latest 21st-Century, high-technology testing.

Pepsi-Cola, for example, fully produces multiple big-budget commercials for each one it's going to ultimately run so they can use a technique called BehaviorScan "to pipe different TV ads to different households in test markets in Eau Claire, Wis., and Cedar Rapids, Iowa" and then "[measure] those ads against the households' actual purchase activity to see if the commercials work."

MasterCard USA spent five years—time enough to earn a bachelor's and master's degree—developing its own computer modeling system "that can assess the effects of hundreds of variables."

Of course, proprietary computer-modeling systems that can assess the effects of hundreds of variables aren't particularly new. Or particularly accurate, for that matter. In the 1980s, the Club of Rome used one to predict that by now the world would be filled shoulder-to-shoulder with starving people. And another model, which predicted that manmade global warming would melt the icecaps by 2013, is having a hard time explaining why those icecaps have grown to record size and why temperatures have been cooling for 15 straight years.

But the real mega *muda* of this whole process is the loss of great ideas. As *BusinessWeek* writes:

> Remember all the millennium talk of innovative new ways to reach consumers? With caution now the watchword, many marketers have put those ideas on the back burner. Any groundbreaking ads or new products are vulnerable to instant veto..." There's huge research before anything goes anywhere," laments Cheryl Berman, chairman and chief creative officer of ad agency Leo Burnett USA. "A housewife in Ohio can make or break a new product or ad concept. It's cowardly, but people are afraid of taking a risk."[15]

We could go on and on like a testing cycle about all the different kinds of *muda* that may be lurking around your marketing department or agency, but the best person to find it is you. In his book, *Up the*

Organization, Robert Townsend, the Avis CEO who turned the company around and hired Doyle Dane Bernbach, recommended the perfect way to do this. He called it the Man from Mars technique. If you were a visiting man from Mars, and you saw something that didn't make sense to you, you wouldn't take anything for granted because you were from 49 million miles away. You'd ask an earthling to explain it.

As part of the constant questioning that leads to more and more improvement, it's important to throw out preconceived notions, throw out history and experience, and approach everything you see as if you were a man from Mars. When you see something that doesn't make sense—and sooner or later you will—ask why it's done that way. And if the answer you get is no more enlightening than that's how it's always been done, you know you've struck a mother lode of *muda*.

So far, we've talked about eliminating many forms of waste from your advertising process. The Lean Agency eliminates *muda* by:

- Gearing for customer pull, not peak demand.
- Making the work flow smoothly and continuously, not through stops, starts and revisions.
- Adding only those steps which add value.
- Building, rather than trying to inspect, quality in. This means replacing top-heavy hierarchies that exist to critique the work with empowered, cross-functional teams under decisive leaders who coach instead of bossing.
- Knocking down both emotional and physical walls between different functions.
- Eliminating support functions which encourage laxity and irresponsibility.
- Trusting in good people's ability to do what's right, not forcing them to conform to top-down systems, standards and controls.
- Evaluating the work by tangible results rather than by the number of standardized tasks completed.
- Recognizing that creation is a reactional process, not a transactional one.

Brand Advertising

- In meetings, with team actions and through suggestion programs, constantly striving for improvement.
- Making all information visually available.
- Constant conducting sessions to devise ways to improve the work and ferret out *muda*.
- Encouraging suggestions by requiring fast, no-baloney responses.
- Celebrating success while learning from, instead of punishing, interesting or aggressive failures.

But eliminating waste isn't necessarily the same as adding value. It depends on, among other things, what your organization is building.

Lean Production has done wonders for Toyota, but do you want your agency to become the Toyota of advertising? It's a trick question, so think before you answer. Toyota builds lower-cost, fuel-efficient, trouble-free, bread-and-butter cars and trucks. They don't, however, build inspiring, soul-stirring ones. Toyota Camrys are popular, all right, but nowhere near as cherished as, say, the first Ford Mustang, the Nissan 240ZX, most years' Corvettes, Jeep CJ-7s (later Wranglers), both the old Austin and new BMW Mini-Coopers and both the old and new VW Beetles. A Toyota Camry doesn't stand out from all the other cars on the road. It doesn't attract consumers' attention and interest and make drivers of other cars hunger to buy one. Your advertising has to; otherwise consumers won't buy your product.

So the Lean Agency has to go beyond eliminating waste. Eliminating waste is an accomplishment, all right, but it's one of eliminating a negative. The Lean Agency must also add a positive accomplishment: creating value with superior ideas. And, as you'll see from the next chapter, that calls for a different, very special, way of thinking.

Chapter Six
The shortest distance between Point A and Point B isn't necessarily the fastest way to get there.

Ever go on-line for driving directions? The software usually gives you a choice between the shortest route and the fastest route. In advertising, as in driving, the two are anything but synonymous.

Fat Agencies operate on the high-school geometry principle that the shortest distance between two points is a straight line. Though it may appear efficient, their straight-line approach is more suited to proving high-school geometry theorems than to creating advertising that adds substantial value to clients' brands.

For one thing, this kind of straight line is not the shortest distance. In fact, it's not all that straight. Its very nature induces all kinds of stops, starts, holds, revisions and other detours. And even if it were the shortest, fastest route, it still wouldn't be the best way to get there. Because it filters out too many good ideas too early—or prevents them from even being thought of.

Fat Agencies sincerely believe that they give clients more effective advertising faster if they narrow down the direction of the work as early in the process as possible. So the process is devoted to quickly picking a small number of workable concepts, usually built around one perspective or strategy.

Like all development processes, this one starts with some new development in the marketplace. Maybe the client has a new product, or an improvement on an existing product, or a line extension. Maybe there's a new competitor, or a change in market share, or some kind of change in pricing. Maybe there's some kind of new health information that a food brand can capitalize on. Or maybe it's just another new model year for an automotive brand.

Whatever the development, the client defines and explains it to the agency. The agency—usually just its department or group heads—will then analyze the client information, devise a strategy, set final and interim due dates. The agency managers will establish a sequence of tasks, assign people to perform them and others to track the completion status. Only then will they turn the assignment over to the people who actually carry it out. But first, they'll put constraints on them.

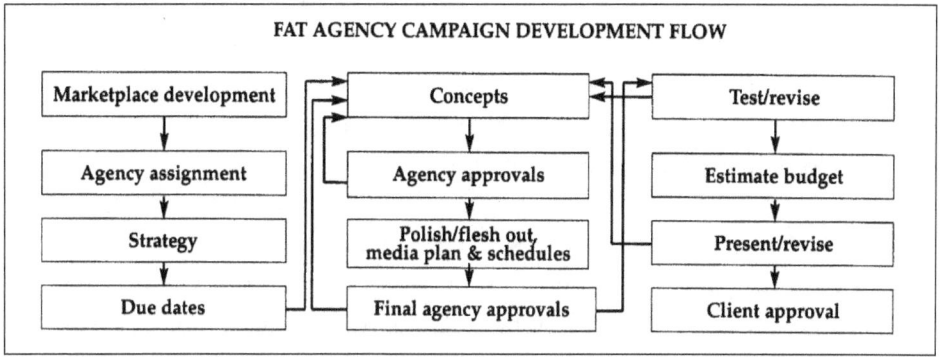

The first constraint is making the direction flow down from the top. The generals set the overall boundaries of the client's problem and its solution at the outset, in terms just specific enough to be confining, and then leave the troops to fill in the blanks as best they can.

The second constraint is on who's allowed to fill in those blanks—and who isn't. "Agencies have done little to change the way they create advertising," says Graham Phillips, a former chairman-CEO of Ogilvy & Mather and Young & Rubicam, who should know. "Currently, a team of agency people and the client develop strategy. After a great deal of time and money has been spent, the task is handed to a few creative people. . . . Usually, the rest of the team and the client are excluded from the development of creative work. As a result, first creative efforts are often wide of the mark, causing more delays."[16]

And that's because of the third constraint— scheduling and budgeting the process as if it were a straight-line process, which it isn't. A straight line is one-dimensional, with length but not width. It's too narrow to allow working on different parts of the solution side by side. You can't even start on Step 5 until you have satisfactory results from Step 4. At the very least, this builds in delay. Like the moving object in Newton's Laws of Motion, the straight-line process keeps moving in the same direction unless acted upon by an outside force. And that force is unlikely to be Fat Agency management. Even if that same direction is wrong, they fear that starting over will take too long and cost too much. Which it very well might, because the farther creative teams travel along the same line, the more of an emotional commitment to the direction they build up. So, like a modern supertanker or a Civil War infantry division on the march, changing direction is very, very slow, gradual and difficult.

The fourth constraint is making the process totally consecutive. The straight line narrows not only how many functional parts of the campaign you can address at the same time, but also how wide a range of ideas you're allowed to consider for each part.

In theory, the straight-line approach's consecutive nature saves time and money because it focuses relatively few concepts on one perspective or strategy, then narrows them down quickly and puts the bulk of the remaining effort into fleshing out and polishing the survivors.

In practice, it saves neither. Following a flawed plan until something goes wrong and only then repeating previous steps usually makes the work late, over budget and less than brilliant. So Fat Agencies constantly deceive themselves and constantly fall farther and farther behind a growing number of revision cycles.

By its very nature, the straight-line process generates pressure to meet due dates, and this pressure causes many potentially good ideas to not even be explored. Fat Agencies constantly whine about how their clients shoot down good ideas without realizing how many good ideas their own straight-line process aborts. Creativity depends on uncertainty, which linear systems don't handle too well. You can't build uncertainty into straight-line planning. Unless you're like the Duke of Medina-Sedonia, who, as admiral of a Spanish Armada plagued with leaky ships, untrained crews, polluted drinking water and adverse winds and tides, wrote his king that "we sail forth in the confident expectation of a miracle."

It would be bad enough if all that linear systems did was put Fat Agencies at the bottom of deep holes and encourage them to keep digging. But what's worse is a fifth constraint, which excludes the people who pay for the work, on whose behalf it's being done, and who usually have more insight into the brand (and into its audiences and its marketplace position) than anyone in Fat Agency management—the clients. To Fat Agencies, the client is at worst an adversary and at best a bull in the china shop. The biggest right that a Fat Agency bestows upon its clients is usually the right to remain silent. No sooner does a client bring a Fat Agency into the loop than the Fat Agency starts working to cut the client out of it—meeting valid inputs and insights with, at best, bored tolerance, and urgent disaster-checks on the progress of campaigns that have drop-dead launch dates with vaguely upbeat reassurances.

This perception of clients as people with pockets but not brains is why Fat Agencies invest most of their resources on the *muda* end of campaign development. They're typically light on creating concepts; often ten to twelve campaign ideas quickly narrowed down to three finalists (one of which is the agency's darling) will do. And because clients are seen as dumb enough to be fooled by packaging, Fat Agencies will be disproportionately heavy on fleshing out the finalists (and particularly the agency darling) with additional ad executions, fully written body copy, beautifully designed layouts, nearly finished photo images, perfectly set type and other production values which just *have* to dazzle the client into buying the campaign concept.

The word "darling" may sound strange in this context, but it reflects the straight-line, consecutive process' dirty little secret. And that's that, like Pygmalion, good creatives become emotionally involved with their handiwork. Somewhere along the line from a blank piece of paper (or computer screen) to tight, polished comps, a funny thing usually happens. The creatives fall in love. They come upon a concept they feel is innovative. Exciting. Capable of attracting notice, winning awards and maybe even getting the cash register to ring. And they unconsciously pledge their troth to it, forsaking all others. That doesn't mean that they won't honestly try to come up with others, but after they've fallen in love, they're just going through the motions. Once their darling is masking-taped up to the wall along with a half-dozen or so other tissues, they keep coming back to it. They start finding it harder and harder to develop more alternative concepts. It becomes emotionally difficult for them to even think of, much less consider, other ideas which may be even more powerful. After all, the Fat Agency straight-line process wants them to come up with the one idea and wants them to do so in a hurry. So why shouldn't they stop once their guts tell them they've found it?

Fat Agencies honestly believe that shortening the steps streamlines the entire process, but it doesn't. Widening the process does, even though the process and its component steps may look more complicated and convoluted.

In the automotive industry, for example, Toyota and its main parts supplier, Nippondenso, don't streamline tasks; they actually seem to complicate them. They explore substantially more different ideas than their competitors do along the way. Yet, they're up to twice as fast as the competition, never miss launch dates or interim milestones, and have the best product quality in the industry. Toyota launches more new models each year than any other carmaker in the world with about one-fourth the number of engineers Detroit uses on a car project. And making cars is much harder, more expensive and more complicated than making ads.

Like Toyota and Nippondenso, the Lean Agency follows a wide, concurrent process instead of a consecutive, straight-line approach. Instead of rushing to arrive at the best of a few concepts based on one overall strategy, it continually evaluates and reevaluates many alternatives based on many different strategic perspectives. It doesn't hand down "design specs" from the top, but rather lets them emerge throughout the process as its teams explore different approaches to different parts of the solution. It distributes the planning and control to the people who can best understand and react to interim concepts as they develop, because those are the people—in creative, in media, in marketing or account planning—who are developing them.

And these people include the generals in among the combat troops. Through the 18th Century, military commanders led their armies from the front—not just to inspire the troops with their personal bravery, but to be able to see with their own eyes what was going on on the front in time to instantly react to it. By the time of the Napoleonic Wars, armies had grown too big, and fronts too extended, to make that possible. So generals led from rear headquarters, using maps and secondhand, delayed reports from aides-de-camp on horseback. Today, with helicopters, satellites, AWACS planes and Predator drones; with digital communications and real-time, computerized battle maps, commanders can be at the front no matter where they are physically and can make tactical decisions based on what's really happening right now.

Before Toyota builds cars or trucks, they build sets of possibilities to satisfy the customer's needs, arriving at a final solution by a combination of narrowing and widening. They narrow by breaking the problem down into components and creating different alternatives for each. They widen by increasing the number of alternatives and the number and type of people who search for and converge on the solution.

Narrowing down to parts of the problem widens the range of overall solutions to converge on. Here's how it works. Let's say a bicycle company is trying to design three new bike models. It can limit its creativity to three complete bikes. Or it can develop three alternative ways to make each of a bike's main components—the frame, the drive, the wheel sets, the suspensions, the brakes. In the first case, it ends up with three bicycles; in the second, with 243 bicycle combinations. Which way do you think is more likely to develop the best new bikes? Right.

Consecutive Bicycle Development	**Concurrent Bicycle Development**
	3 frames
	3 drives
	3 wheel sets
	3 brakes
	3 suspensions
3 bicycles	243 combinations

In a way, marketing and advertising creativity work like Internet connections. Fat Agencies operate with the equivalent of a 56K dial-up modem. Less comes through, more slowly, because the pipeline is so confined. Lean Agencies operate more like a cable or optic fiber line. More comes through, faster, because the unconfined pipeline has so much more room for it.

Broadband Creativity is the opposite of confinement.

To begin with, it's not confined to one strategy. It starts with a defined problem or objective, and the strategies emerge from the executions.

The team working on those executions isn't confined to the creative team, though the creatives do play a big role. Instead, initial concepting is done by the creatives, the media planner, the account or marketing person, perhaps the print or broadcast producer and maybe—heresy of heresies—some of the clients themselves. Graham Phillips asks, "Why not keep the entire team and the client involved in the idea-generating phase?" Broadband Creativity says, "Why not, indeed!"

It's not confined to one perspective. Marshaling lots of skills and talents from people in different disciplines teamed together forces them to continually develop and evaluate the work from different perspectives. So many high-quality ideas emerge so quickly that it looks like magic. But it's not; it's just excellence. Management doesn't have to hover over the process pushing the standards because the very environment pulls excellence out of people—bottom-up, not top-down.

This emphasis on many solutions from many perspectives needn't be confined to advertising agencies. According to David Frum, America's first MBA President brought this kind of thinking into one of the least likely bastions of leanness, the executive branch of the federal government:

> Bush's guiding philosophy in so many areas of politics was this: There were other ways of entering a room than charging headfirst through the wall. It was not always a betrayal of principle to knock politely at the door.
>
> Bush had another guiding principle, and it helped to explain many of the foreign-policy actions that irked his conservative supporters: He would not commit himself to any one course of action until he must. If Colin Powell wanted to try a diplomatic solution to a problem—and Donald Rumsfeld promised to have a military solution ready to go in three weeks—Bush would not say, "Right—we're doing it Don's way." He would say: "Colin you have three weeks."

Like the White House process, Broadband Creativity isn't confined to a process of elimination. Instead, it's a process of searching for and converging on the solution.

It's not confined to just a few ideas. Broadband Creativity works to generate a large number of ideas over a relatively short period of time. And it's not confined to good ideas. Everything—the good, the bad and the ugly—gets scribbled onto paper and masking-taped to the wall.

Where the individual ideas can be sorted in to groups of shared concepts and directions. Where ideas can be mixed and matched. Where ways to strengthen one idea by, say, combining it with parts of another become more readily apparent. And where some of the turkeys trigger ideas that evolve into swans.

It's not confined to any set of formal processes or procedures. Like water, the work finds its own path to flow. And, like white water through a canyon, it flows quickly. You'd expect no less from a process based on continuous-flow and just-in-time creation. The Doyle Dane Bernbach revolution of the 1960s emphasized adding time to the creative process, so that the creative team would have time to give the project enough thought to make it right. Maybe so. But, paradoxically, most people in advertising, regardless of specialty, are at their best and most creative as time runs out. Give them weeks, and they'll take weeks—with relatively little to show for the time until the final day or two (see Parkinson's Law). As the clock runs down, the adrenaline starts to flow, and that's when miracles happen. Good teams and good creatives have shown themselves over and over to be capable of creating literally dozens of big ideas in a matter of days, not weeks. So why not start the process with days, not weeks, to go?

Here's an overview of how it works.

	FAT AGENCY	**LEAN AGENCY**
Idea Process	Straight-line	Broadband
Concepts	1-3	Many
Perspectives/ Strategies	1	Many
Leadership	Administrative	Expertise/coaching
Staffing	Departmentalized	Inclusive
Management style	Based on inflexible tasks	Based on flexible results
Specifications	Handed down in initial assignment	Emerge throughout process
Responsibility	Managers order, workers do	Individual excellence/ personal responsibility
Time frame	Choose fast, polish long	More time creating, no polishing
Improvement focus	Systems, structure	Products, work

Brand Advertising

A Lean Agency team meets with a client or client team and discusses challenges and objectives. They gather as much factual information as they can about the brand, the audience, the competition, the marketplace. They study it. During this initial meeting, they start to get ideas. To spot potential problems. To get everyone on board. And to start winning client buy-in.

And then the fun begins.

They come together and spend a half-day or so generating ideas. The idea here is not who develops which idea, but rather to work together, to support instead of backstab, and to develop all the ideas further.

Every idea gets written down. No idea gets criticized or mocked or discarded. Many, however, get built on.

Then, the creative team takes all the pieces of paper on which all the ideas to date are written down. They retreat to their own work areas and spread the ideas out on a wall or big table. They stare at them. They talk about them. They find a compelling nugget in a confusing line. They change visuals. They mix and match.

And then the team meets again. They put all the ideas up on the wall. They physically group the ideas around common themes, benefits and marketing directions. Maybe they name each direction and write out the name on a title page. They look for areas they haven't addressed. They shift some of the ideas from one group to another. Maybe they combine two or more groups that have a lot in common. Maybe they combine two or more ideas. They come up with more ideas to fill the holes they've identified. They look at ideas that aren't quite working and figure out how to help them.

Finally, the creatives (mainly the art director) will take a day or two to lay out all the ideas as roughs—one to a page, roughly sketched or downloaded low-resolution images that simply convey the idea, all headlines in the same simple font, and so on. Just tight enough to convey the idea, but not so tight as to be wasting time and money.

And that's when the process of elimination starts, with the client decision-makers part of the team. Together, the Lean Agency and the client will go through all the ways the team could think of to meet the client objectives or fulfill the strategy. These ideas will all be in clear but rough form (usually headlines and freehand sketches), before too much financial or emotional investment has gone into any one approach. All the work will be there, unscreened and unedited. Together, the Lean Agency and the client will compare all the ideas. To each other. To the strategy. To what the competitors are doing. They'll analyze the ideas, group them, combine them, discover parts of the strategy that the executions don't cover. They'll see which ones are just plain wrong, either from a factual or a marketing standpoint. Together, they'll discuss what makes the good ideas work and why, discarding as many concepts as possible along the way.

Sometimes the agency-client team will learn some new facts. Or work their way into a new strategic approach that invalidates much of the work already done. Maybe the agency will have to start over a second or third time.

No problem. It only takes another week or so to get the work on its new track. And the final campaign will be sharper and more focused—to say nothing of getting done faster and cheaper—than if a Fat Agency had developed it in secret, the straight-line way, then sprung it on the client at the last minute.

Fat Agencies view client participation at this point as fatal, but to a Lean Agency, it's vital. For one thing, clients have brains as well as pockets, and they just might come up with something good that no one else has thought of. Or maybe they'll tell you that you don't need that ad campaign to recruit vacationers to the website you're redoing, because they already have tons of consumer traffic referred by wholesalers, and the problem isn't traffic volume but closing ratio. Or that that concept with the image of a train wreck won't go down well in the UK, where derailments on the privatized British Rail system have prompted angry headlines and questions in Parliament.

But best of all, the clients will start to take a sense of ownership in the work. This sense of ownership breeds a comfort level in work they'd reject out of hand if it were presented to them cold. This is why Lean Agencies very often find themselves selling their most adventurous, most unconventional, but solidly grounded concepts far more easily. And, having sold them, can concentrate on getting the body copy, the image, the brand look and page design just right. (With television concepts, which come out as storyboards with rough key visuals only and a video-audio script, they can then start looking at directors' reels and putting together budgets.)

Now, all this may bear a superficial resemblance to the Fat Agency idea process that the Doyle Dane Bernbach revolution established in the 1960s. But its has some very fundamental differences.

First, the ideas are generated by a team, not just a creative team. The copywriter and art director will probably come up with more of the ideas, and they'll play a vital role in making other team members' ideas work, but they won't monopolize the thinking.

Second, the emphasis is on generating as many ideas consistent with the strategy or objective as possible. So, third, there will be no judgment, no negative criticism of concepts (no matter how awful), no editing, no narrowing down. As a result, there will be few, if any, blind alleys. Mainly because the process discourages falling in love with any specific ideas which may turn into blind alleys which the agency has gone too far down to quickly and easily turn back.

Fourth, the process is exploratory, not prescriptive. It's not about polishing and fleshing out any one campaign so that the client will be too dazzled by its glare to reject it.

And finally, the client decision-makers are team members in good standing. Not necessarily all the way through the process, but enough to see all the rough ideas, including the real stinkers, and then join in narrowing them down to a solution that everyone can buy into.

All the foregoing may sound like an oversimplification, but Broadband Creativity really works the way it sounds. One of the projects we applied it to was an ad campaign introducing Invensys Software Systems (ISS). Invensys is a multinational, multibillion-dollar company that sells controls and control systems to industry. They had just merged six software companies they'd acquired (Baan, Foxboro, Wonderware, APV Systems, CAPS Logistics, and Invensys CRM) into a new division selling to mass manufacturers. The manufacturers all had factory automation. They all had e-commerce, supply-chain and customer relationship management (CRM) software. The problem was that many of these systems had been purchased at different times, at different levels of the organization chart, to achieve different objectives. Many of the systems worked at different speeds—the e-commerce software sucking in orders as fast as customers could key them in on the Internet, for example, with the

Brand Advertising

automation software working at the speed of the factory's slowest machine. To make matters worse, many of the individual software systems came from different IT companies, had different architectures and spoke different languages.

ISS asked us to create an ad campaign based on how an older, slower manufacturing automation system can bottleneck fast-moving e-commerce. Applying Broadband Creativity, we came up with about a dozen rough ideas in a few days.

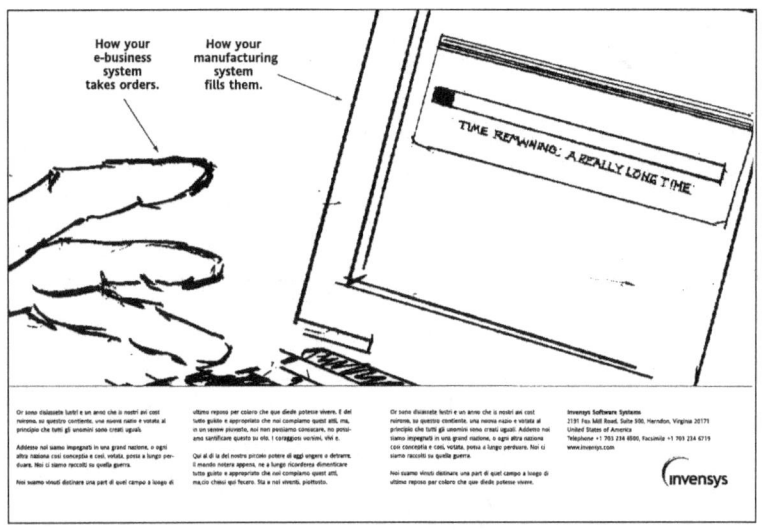

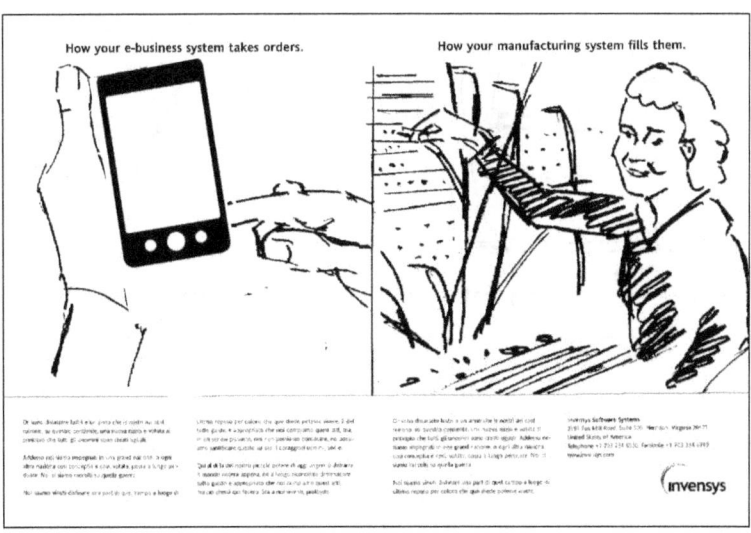

Brand Advertising

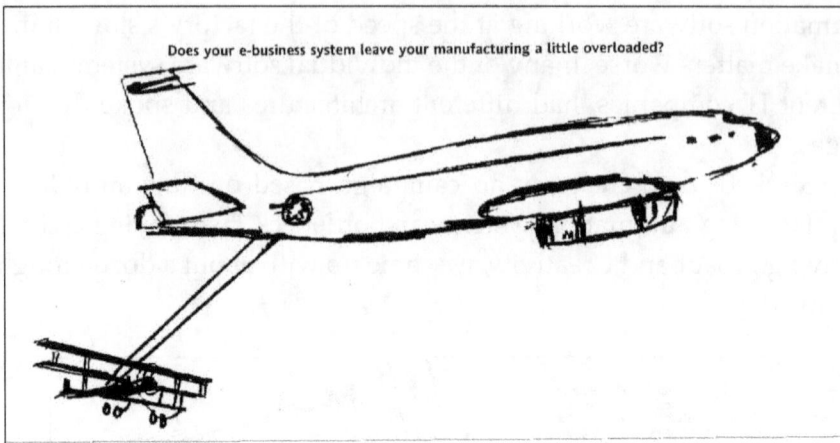

Brand Advertising

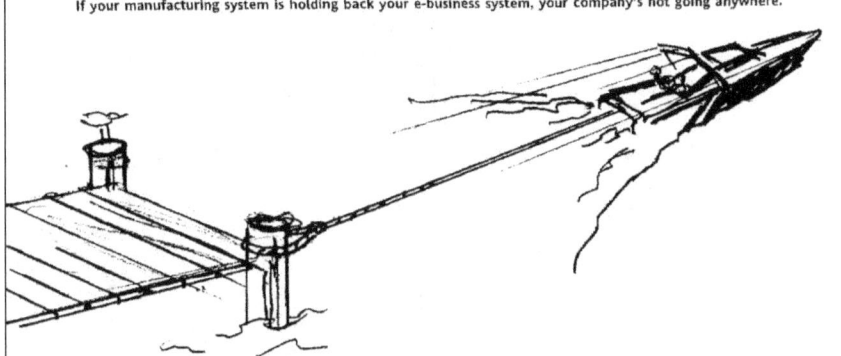

Brand Advertising

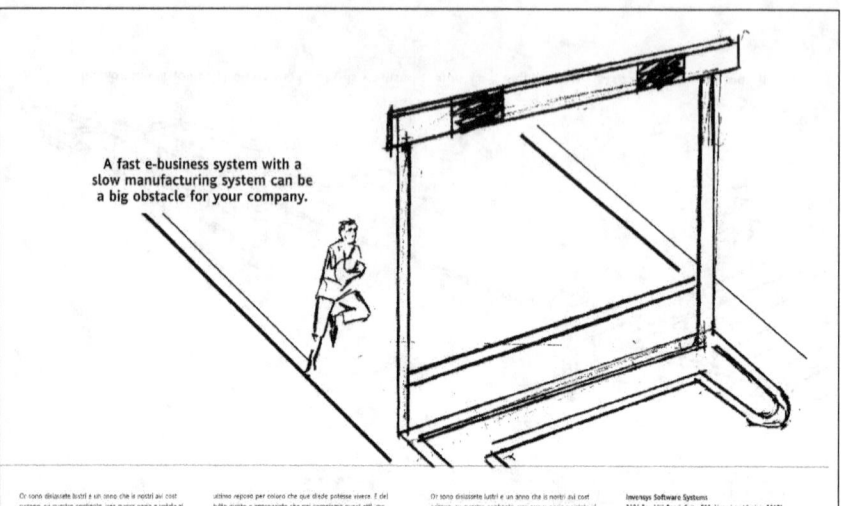

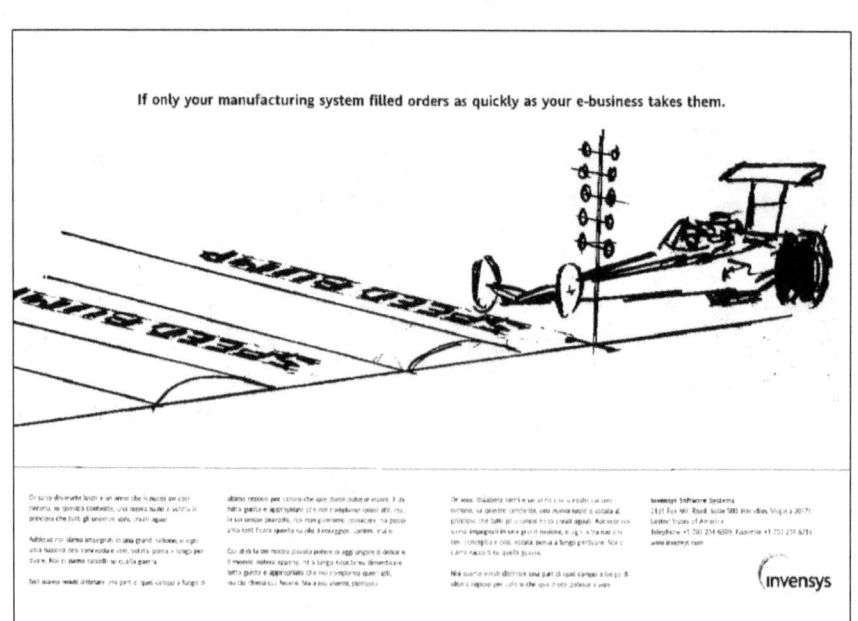

Brand Advertising

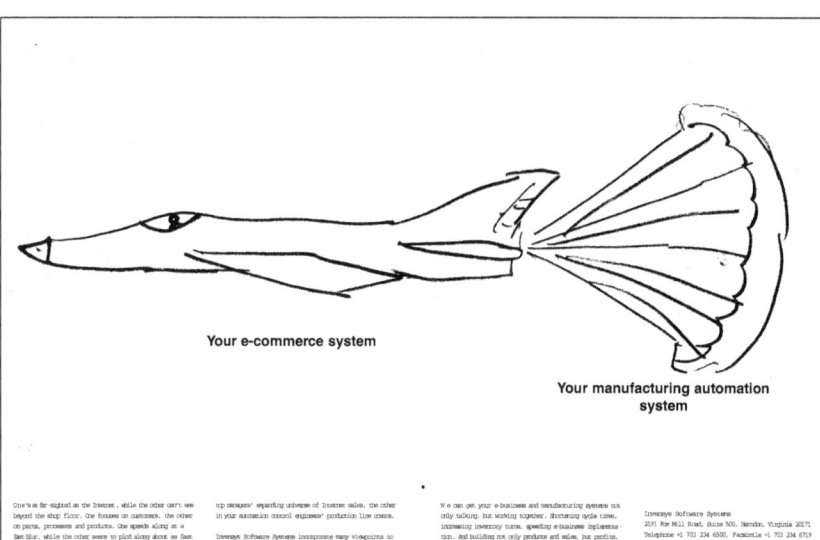

Brand Advertising

Seeing them crystallized the client's strategy—and showed them that it was wrong. The speed difference was only the tip of the iceberg. The iceberg itself was the basic incompatibility of different systems, with different functions, bought at different times by different executives to do different things at different speeds, with no ability to even talk to each other. ISS realized it could sell patches that would give disparate software systems the ability to talk to each other and work and play well together. These patches would cost customers far less than whole new systems and entail little, if any, factory downtime—but they would make ISS more money than dealing with just automation and e-commerce. So the strategy shifted to identifying the disconnect between a manufacturer's different software systems and showing how ISS could overcome it.

We sat down, and after another day or two of Broadband Creativity, these concepts emerged.

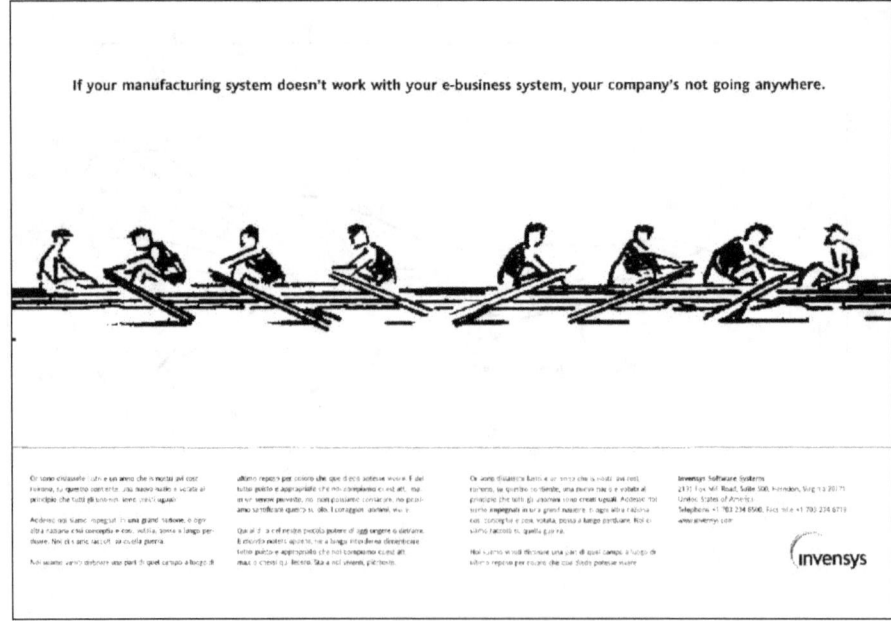

Brand Advertising

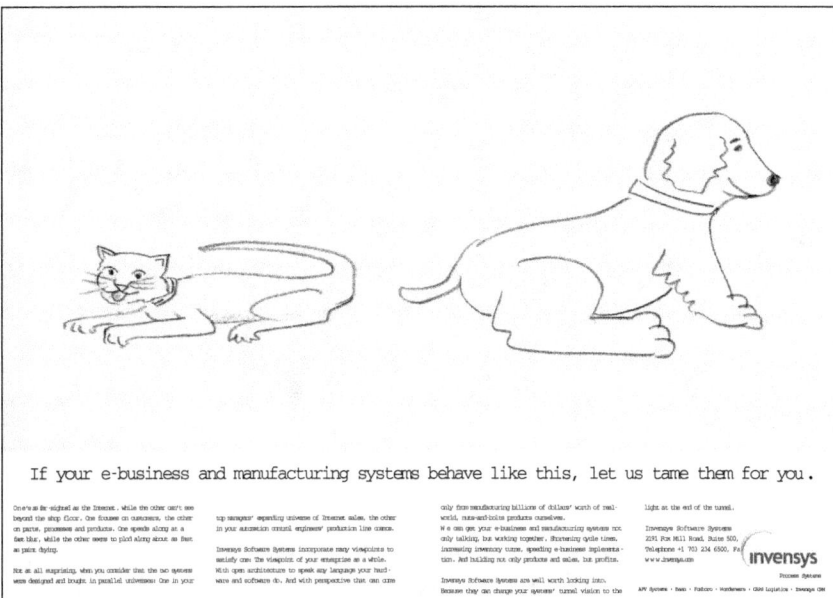

If your e-business and manufacturing systems behave like this, let us tame them for you.

If your e-business and manufacturing systems aren't on the same song sheet, let us get them in harmony.

Brand Advertising

If this reminds you of your e-business and manufacturing systems, let us get them playing the same game.

If this reminds you of your e-business and manufacturing systems, let us get them pulling in the same direction.

Brand Advertising

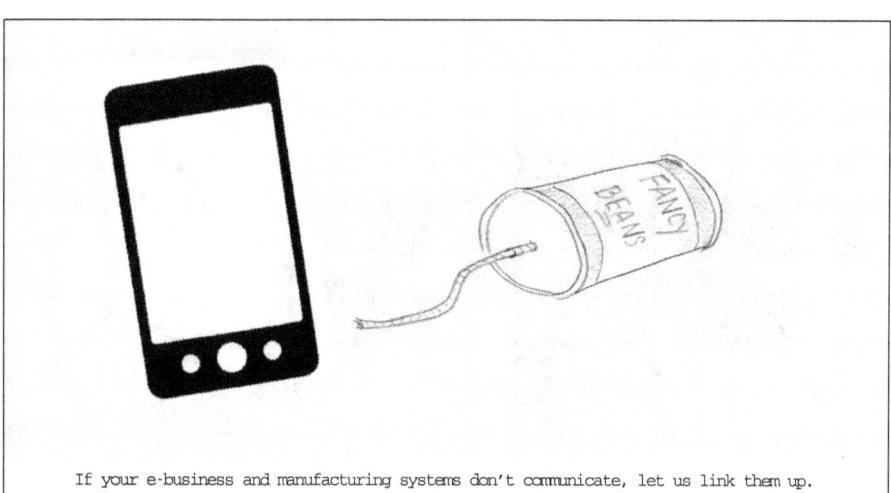

Brand Advertising

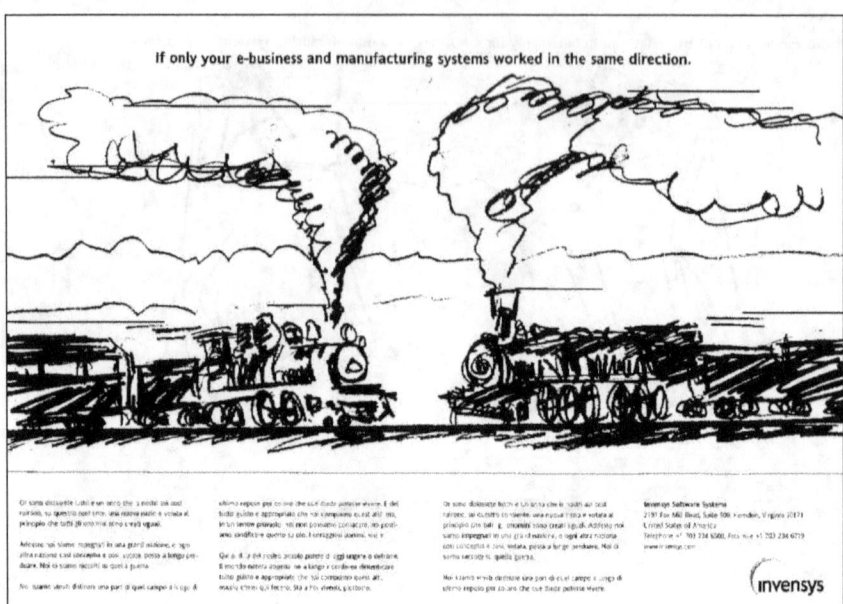

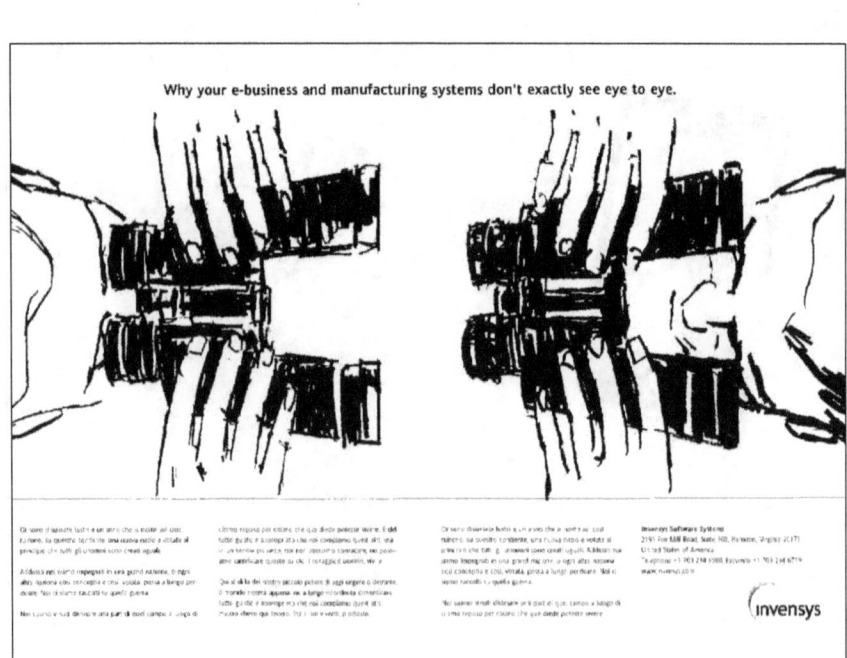

Brand Advertising

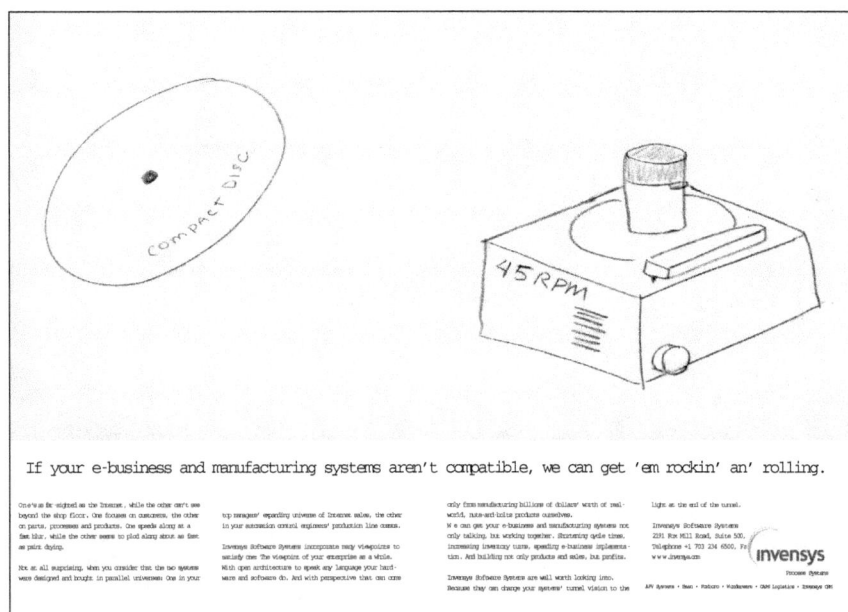

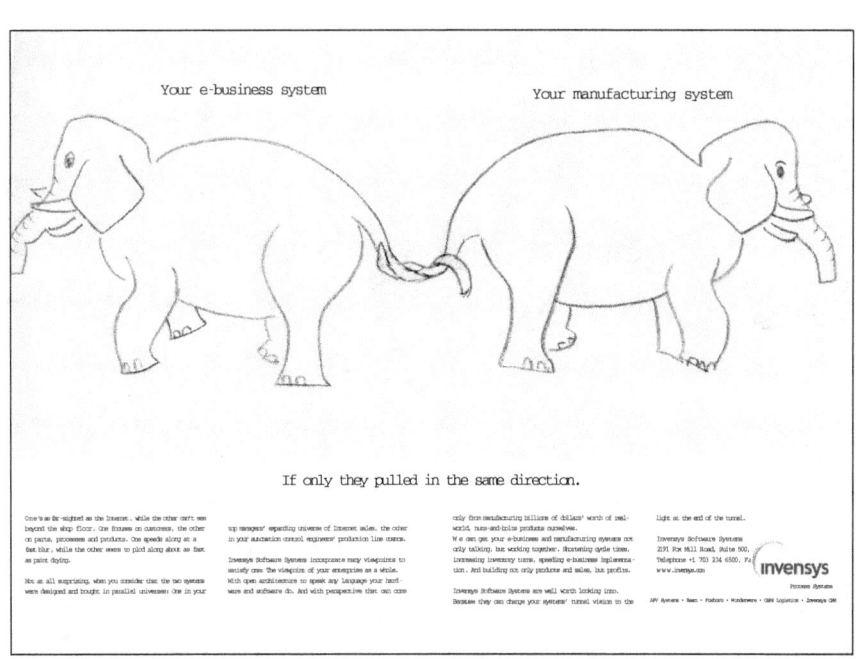

Brand Advertising

Brand Advertising

Three of these became the final campaign, though they weren't done as a campaign. Let's repeat that. Though they were concepted as one-shots, not parts of a campaign, they work as a campaign. Imposing campaign consistency criteria at this stage of Broadband Creativity only adds a constraint. And it's an unnecessary constraint. The process, focused on a common strategy or objective, generating ideas from smart, talented people, assures not only effectiveness, but also consistency. Part of this consistency comes from the common focus. Part will come from common visual elements—layout, type handling, logo, tone of voice, and so on.

As you can see, the ISS clients made good choices. But they could have made equally good choices by selecting other ideas and combining them into a campaign. In fact, that's what they ended up doing. The train-wreck concept was originally one of their three final choices. Then, for reasons discussed earlier, they had to discard it. They went back to the concept pool and picked another idea that was consistent and just as good. Which is part of the beauty of the whole process.

These ads ran in *Industry Week, CIO, Chief Executive, Managing*

Brand Advertising

Automation, and *Darwin* magazines. In all four, they achieved record high readership scores. Two of the magazines liked the ads so much, they upgraded them to premium inside-cover position at no extra charge. And that record number of readers apparently liked what they saw. During the course of the campaign, ISS went from a $400 million loss to overall profitability. We're not saying that our ads were completely responsible for this turnaround. But they did get lots of prospects thinking about and talking to ISS, and that never hurts.

You've just seen a lot of work. What you can't see, and will have to take our word for, is how little time it took to do it. Broadband Creativity sessions go quickly. In fact, cleaning up the scribbled ideas to make them legible enough for presentation can often take a day or two more than thinking them up.

So if Broadband Creativity is such a fast, cheap, more foolproof, less painful way of producing more effective advertising, why don't more agencies practice it? Well, it's like the old story about the formula for turning lead into gold: you have to follow the recipe under the light of a full moon without thinking of the word "rhinoceros." Which is much harder than it sounds.

Broadband Creativity works only when you mix in its four key ingredients: the people, the leadership, the process, and the control system. Fat Agencies can muster, at best, one or two of them.

The first ingredient—people—means hiring people who are outstanding at what they do but secure enough to realize that others, outside their specialty, may from time to time come up with ideas to help them do what they do even better. Fat Agencies can do this.

The second—leadership—means selecting leaders who work on the front line. Leaders whose decisions are followed because they're even better at what they do than the other team members—not obeyed because they come from someone in a corner office with a fancy title. Fat Agencies might be able to do this, but their culture, hierarchy and straight-line systems work against effective front-line leaders staying very long.

The third key ingredient—process—is a commitment to Lean Advertising. To clearing away the hierarchies, systems, structures and, most important, the *muda*.

The fourth is the control system, or, more properly, the lack-of-control system. The agency must abandon top-down hierarchy for responsibility distributed throughout the organization, particularly to the people who are doing the actual work. It must stop focusing on structures, systems and steps, and start focusing on results. Instead of controls and measurements to keep the troops in line, the agency should maintain a results-based environment where incompetence and laziness stand out like a sore thumb and will be tolerated about as much as Rush Limbaugh at a NOW meeting.

By definition, Fat Agencies can't or won't take either of the last two steps. That's why they're not Lean Agencies. It's like going on a diet. There's nothing extremely difficult to do and nothing tangible preventing anyone from doing it. But as the current obesity statistics will tell you, most overweight people just don't. Same thing with Fat Agencies. Changing over doesn't require news skills, new tools, new computers or other capital investments, or new methodologies. It does require a major re-emphasis of the fundamental skills that the agency exists to offer clients and hired its people for in the first place. But just as Moses said to the Israelites about the Law:

> . . . it is not hidden from you and it is not distant. It is not in heaven, [for you] to say, "Who can ascend to the heaven for us and take it for us, so that we can listen to it and perform it? Nor is it across the sea, [for you] to say, "Who can cross to the other side of the sea for us and take it for us, so that we can listen to it and perform it?" Rather, the matter is very near to you in your mouth and in your heart to perform it.[18]

In other words, there's nothing tangible preventing Fat Agencies from making the transition to Lean Agencies. But because of a whole bunch of stupid intangibles, most will never even try.

Chapter Seven
Why Fat Agencies stay that way.

In the previous chapter, we touched on an ancient formula for transforming lead into gold. What made it impossible to follow successfully was that once you know you're not supposed to think of the word "rhinoceros," it's impossible not to. In other words, the mental part.

For a widget manufacturer transitioning to Lean Production, there are lots of purely physical considerations: rearranging assembly lines, cleaning up and lighting the factory floor, possibly replacing heavy machinery, reconfiguring supply and delivery chains, going from standard inventory controls to pull-scheduling, setting up instant visual communications systems, and so on. Most manufacturers who try this part of Lean Transformation accomplish it. In fact, with the right vision and commitment, many manufacturers we know of successfully transformed themselves all the way.

But for some manufacturers, and for most Fat Agencies (which, being people and service businesses, don't have all these physical considerations to cope with), the transition founders over mental issues.

The first of these issues is failure to even recognize the need to change anything. In the 1960s, Robert Townsend wrote that it's human nature to learn from failures, not successes. When something goes wrong, we usually agonize over it until we find out what caused the failure and how to correct it. But success prompts no such questioning. We assume it's because everything we're doing is exactly right—even when our success results solely from the high tide of a rising economy lifting our leaky boat.

Things haven't changed much since then. In a televised 2003 speech, Peter Drucker said that companies which have been doing well for years resist change. Right or wrong, their answers have been working, so their culture avoids questions. Fat Agencies have been successful, by and large, because they've been competing against other Fat Agencies. There's no Toyota of the advertising industry. Yet. So they just loosen their belts, pull down their ties, open their collar buttons, and never raise those awkward questions.

It may take a sense of crisis, real or perceived, to get Fat Producers off the dime. Fat Agencies, working the same way as the Fat Agencies they compete with, don't have that sense of crisis. If they're striking out in one new business pitch after another, if their payrolls are filled with equivalents of the Napoleonic artilleryman who held the horses, if they're flushing thousands of dollars down the toilet making supertight comps to dazzle the clients into buying mediocre ideas, if they're working on full 15 percent commission plus at least 17.65 percent production markup plus creative, trafficking and other fees and still not making a profit—no big deal, that's business as usual.

But realizing that a Fat Agency needs to become Lean is just the beginning. Its top leaders need to be committed to making changes. It can't be like Quality Circles or Zero Defects or TQM or Six Sigma or any other of those buzzword management fads of the month that get halfheartedly tried for a while and then abandoned for the next fad. The commitment needs to be real, and it needs to be long-term. That's one reason Fat Agency leaders won't make it. Nobel Prize-winning behavioral economist Daniel Kahneman's research explains why: though people think in terms of loss and gain, they think more about the short term than the long term, and fear loss more than they value gain.[19] In other words, they likely lack the guts to risk trying something new and the perseverance to make it stick. To make more than a one-time commitment. To communicate that commitment boldly. To assign the best resources. To demand aggressive milestones. To stay involved. To resist being fooled by people going through the motions until this latest fad goes away.

Sometimes realizing the need for change isn't enough to actually make changes. Wrong as they may be, leaders grow comfortable with the ways they've been doing things over time. The one thing they do realize about change is that it won't be easy. So the first change that may be needed for a Fat Agency to put itself on a diet is a change of leadership. Clients change CEOs and marketing vice presidents when things are going wrong, and the replacements often change advertising agencies. Not as often, agencies that realize things are going wrong change leaders. And while old leadership may be stuck in the "we've always done it that way" rut, new leadership signals change right off the bat. Because, among other things, that's how new leaders make their mark.

Brand Advertising

Whether it's a new leader or an old leader who got religion heading the agency, the first thing he or she needs is a vision of what the new Lean Agency will look like. Instead of departments isolated from each other by unscalably high walls, multifunctional teams will handle specific accounts. The members of these teams will be empowered, their creativity—and we're not referring to just the former creative department—unleashed. Each team will be like a five- or six-person shop, unencumbered by committees and endless meetings, able to make real-time decisions and turn out work on a dime. The process police will be sent off to *gulags*, and layers of bureaucracy turned out to pasture. Great, effective creative work will reign. Clients will be turning backflips because of sales results, while the agency will be needing more wall space just to hang all the awards.

The second thing that leader will need is to make all the advantages of going Lean clear to everyone else. Not to spell out the details of exactly how the new Lean Agency will operate, because that's counterproductive. In order for the transformation to work, its details must be left up to the people who'll have to live and work with them every day.

Which brings us to the next reason why it's difficult to impossible for Fat Agencies to go Lean. In the unlikely event that Fat Agency leaders are capable of making the commitment, they may very well be incapable of making it in the right way. The very nature of Fat Agencies is based on top-down supervision, measurements, standard procedures, controls—all the kiss of death to Lean Agency operations. To make the transition work, top leaders must have a strategic vision of what the agency will move toward and will become. Of how the agency will be different and what advantages these new differences will create. They have to not only keep this strategic vision firmly in mind, but communicate it to the staff, so that it becomes a shared vision that everyone's working toward. And then, having set the high-level vision, they'll need to step back. They'll need to make sure their people know what's expected of them, that they have goals and objectives to shoot for. (These goals could involve, for example, specific reductions in time from assignment to concept, from concept to buy-in, from buy-in to production and placement. Or they could involve such things as number of rough concepts per new campaign, milestones for switching over to mini-agency multifunctional teams, and so on.)

But that's about all they can do from the top. As we've discussed, Lean Producers in any industry create a state of deliberate chaos from which order—actually, different orders, each geared to the specific customer and challenge—emerge. So when a Fat Agency leader says, "We're going Lean" and then follows up with a whole set of fully detailed implementation steps, ways to measure them and controls to make sure each step conforms to the measurements, he's using Fat Agency techniques to establish a state of deliberate order from which chaos will emerge—followed by long, complex, expensive and only marginally effective efforts to eliminate the chaos. In other words, he's defeating the whole changeover from the outset.

Perhaps imposing the changes they believe necessary from the top can transform a relatively small Fat Agency, say less than 75 or 100 employees, but that won't transform it into a Lean Agency. The top-down leader will have to ride close herd on the change process. And long after the change has supposedly been completed, he or she will constantly have to crack the whip to keep the herd of cats on the payroll from straying off in different directions.

So once the vision of change and its fundamental principles come down from the top, how do all the working details of the Lean Agency get built from the bottom? Especially with people from each different discipline approaching the change from their own specific perspectives? Well, it will be better, more effective and more in keeping with the Lean philosophy of pushing decision-making to the people on the line, who are in direct contact with what's going on, to name a team of team leaders, then have them lead their teams in deciding precisely how to turn the vision into reality.

These team leaders must be strong. They must fully and passionately share the company leader's vision of what the new Lean Agency will look like. Together, they must represent all the important functional areas. Individually, they must be respected throughout the agency for the skill and talent they bring to their own respective functions.

Once they're selected, there must be a drop-dead, set-in-stone timetable specifying what has to happen and when the key steps towards change will take place:

Brand Advertising

- When the team leaders will meet and come to consensus on who will be on whose team. (Either the agency leader or an outside consultant/facilitator will chair the meeting at which this consensus is reached. At this meeting the new team leaders will work as a multifunctional team, while the agency leader or outsider will function as team leader.)
- When the team leaders will hold a series of meetings with their new teams to plan the transition – defining team roles, documenting individual responsibilities and discussing procedures for interacting with support services (e.g., media buying [but not planning], accounting, broadcast and print production, IT).
- When and how the team leaders will bring their team members' input to the support team leaders to agree on procedural details, and which individuals will be responsible for documenting the decisions. (During this time the old way of working may continue until the next milestone.)
- When the actual transition will finally arrive—when the physical and psychological walls will come down and individuals from the different disciples will physically

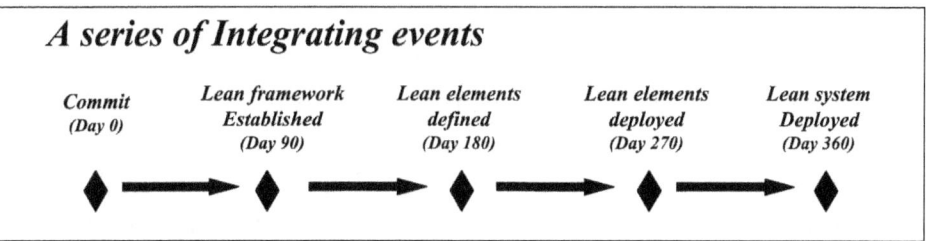

A series of Integrating events

| Commit (Day 0) | Lean framework Established (Day 90) | Lean elements defined (Day 180) | Lean elements deployed (Day 270) | Lean system Deployed (Day 360) |

It makes sense to make the people who will have to live with the new vision day to day responsible for setting the rules and making them work. What better incentive is there for getting things right? It will be impossible for them to point the finger at someone else if something should go awry, and if something does, what doesn't work can be quickly fixed.

After the obvious first steps of identifying and rooting out non-value-added steps, the team of leaders will give the people a more concrete version of the vision and a shove in the right direction to carry it out—putting the responsibility on them to create a new system their own way. Together, they'll both define and implement the changes needed. The team leaders will need to help the people use their knowledge to build from working alternatives as they adopt new working principles and adapt the agency's infrastructure to support them. And they'll do all this the same way they'll lead their teams after the new system is created—with coaching, questioning and ultimate decision-making.

The agency leader has to be patient and persistent while this whole changeover is going on. But he or she must simultaneously be impatient. Impatient with resistance, impatient with foot-dragging, impatient with going through the motions, impatient enough to light a fire under the whole organization until it delivers tangible results. (Of course, if a Fat Agency's leader has been patient with all this *muda* for years, it will take a lot for him or her to start becoming impatient now.)

Needed and potentially constructive as this impatience is, it must be tempered with a healthy dose of realism—particularly regarding how fast to move ahead. The answer will depend largely on the supporting infrastructure's ability to keep up. If the agency has one or two accounts, infrastructure may not be an issue. With six, 10, 20, or more, it definitely is.

The leaders will establish the vision and motivate its implementation. They must make sure their people know that a big change will be necessary and understand that even though this change may go against basic human nature (to guard personal turf), anything less will not be tolerated. They'll have to be benevolent dictators, because people simply aren't going to change out of the goodness in their hearts. Would-be Lean Agency leaders must paradoxically possess two seemingly opposite qualities. They must be strong enough to convince everyone that the transformation *will* proceed along a clearly defined route toward a clearly defined vision—no excuses, no negotiations, no prisoners. But at the same time, they must be empowering enough to give their people and their teams the leeway and the authority necessary to make the transformation happen.

Few Fat Agency leaders have the strength, vision or conviction to do all this. But even if they do, leaders can't make the transition happen all by themselves. Actual implementation depends on department heads and other middle managers, and these supposed supporters of the leadership's vision can actually be its biggest enemies. That's where a potential pitfall lies.

In company after company that's tried to change over from Fat to Lean, it's not the workforce that's had a problem with moving from a structural, command-and-control workplace to an empowered one. It's their managers who feel threatened by what they see as diminution of their own role. Because in a Lean Agency, department heads and managers will have to support the smooth and efficient output of work and the people who actually do it, not the other way around; the marketing communications work itself is what the agency is all about. Among executives who have undergone a Lean Transformation, almost without exception, "concrete heads"—obstructionists who don't want change to take place—are the biggest obstacles.

A small percentage of workers—and a larger proportion of managers—will be unable or unwilling to change work habits that have become as much a part of them as their hairstyle or the clothes they wear. Their extreme discomfort with the new way of working will make them do things from talking the talk but not walking the walk to willfully undermining the transformation.

This is because going from a Fat Agency to a Lean Agency turns everything upside down. Instead of top-down decision-making, there's teamwork and decision-making down the line. Instead of thinking of steps and procedures first, it's customer pull that comes first. That's what makes Toyota the envy of automakers on every continent, but it's also what gives many managers nightmares. So they, more than anyone else in the agency, may need a thorough reorientation. Managers will need to know that they must let go. That they simply will no longer be in a position to give orders. That they'll have to become coaches who let workers take responsibility—even if that means shutting everything down if quality's at risk. That everyone must work together. That the workplace must become participative instead of authoritarian. That what's good for the agency as a whole must come before what's good for any individual.

This goes against most managers' training and experience, to say nothing of the basic human territorial instinct. When empowered teams composed of people who used to work for them take over and start hitting triples and home runs, they're going to feel, at the very least, anxious about the change and concerned that their power has been usurped. So they start waging guerrilla warfare.

We don't know specifically how this happens in Fat Agencies trying to become Lean Agencies, because none, to our knowledge, have even tried the transition yet. But the examples from manufacturing companies are real lulus.

After weeks of planning and conversations with individuals throughout his organization about the coming transformation, the day came for a CEO to brief his entire management team on the details. Marketing, research and development, purchasing, engineering, sales and operations managers from throughout the company were gathered in a hotel ballroom. The CEO stepped forward to speak. His VP of manufacturing and other top executives flanked him on the dais. The intended message of their presence was that everyone in senior management stood behind the move. But it soon became apparent that they didn't. The VP of manufacturing had never argued about going Lean, nor had he voiced any concerns. But he let the entire room know he opposed the plan by rolling his eyes and shaking his head as the CEO outlined certain actions. His body language may have been unconscious, but he clearly let everyone know where he stood. As a result, he severely undermined confidence.

In another company, an operations manager was brought into a catastrophic situation. Productivity was in the basement, expenses were through the roof, production was so backed up that customers were restive. The assembly operation, which normally ran two ten-hour shifts four days a week, was now running around the clock for five, six, sometimes seven days straight. There was so much overtime and time-and-a-half that most workers were too tired out to be interested in making more. Needless to say, the unit was in the red.

The new manager saw immediately that the organization lacked discipline, so he moved quickly to establish authority. He issued a directive that not one decision was to be made, no overtime was to be authorized, and not a purchase order was to be written without his personal approval. Noting that the assembly operation was in disarray, he hired a cadre of supervisors whose job it was to clamp down and keep a tight rein. He met with them daily and issued strict orders. He got tough, fired troublemakers and refused to put up with foolishness. He wore a scowl. Fear spread, and with it came order.

Soon, the situation was no longer out of control. Within three or four months it had stabilized. The backlog was down to a manageable level. The work week was down to four days, where it belonged. The bottom line was now slightly into the black.

This manager deserved a pat on the back, correct? Yes, and he got it. Given the state of affairs when he'd arrived, his actions may have been necessary. His techniques were old school, to say the very least, but he was able to achieve a respectable degree of success.

Then the company leadership decided that, having stabilized the organization and established discipline, the time had come to begin the transformation to Leanness. To reduce layers of management. To push decision-making down to line managers and assembly teams. To replace the authoritarian approach—which had served its purpose if it ever really had been necessary—with teamwork and *esprit de corps* and let them work.

How do you suppose the manager felt about this? As you might expect, his expression didn't resemble one of those smile emojis 😊. But he said he'd do his best. He allowed a Lean Enterprise change agent into the plant, and this change agent began working with one of the production-line cells. Within a couple of weeks this line had made enormous productivity gains.

Soon the operations manager was telling his subordinates to "play along" with the transformation. They were to pretend to be working toward the Lean Transformation—but only while top managers or the change agent were present. Then it would be back to business as usual.

Needless to say, top management was not pleased. But we can understand why he felt as he did. He'd turned around a bad situation in a short time. Even so, the line that had been transformed to continuous flow was producing at a remarkable level. Couldn't he see this?

His CEO went over the figures with him. He grudgingly acknowledged the gain. Top management decided to give him the benefit of the doubt and, with it, another chance. They applauded him for the turnaround and for doing what he felt he must to make it happen. They told him they were convinced that his plant was in position to become a showcase, but only he could make it happen. He now had a model to follow, the line that already had been converted. What was required would be to expand the transformation to the other assembly lines, and eventually throughout every area and department in his plant.

But rumors persisted that he was still sandbagging. He was told that the decision to go Lean had been made at the highest level. It was going to happen; no exceptions would be allowed. His plant would have to be brought into the fold. If specified progress was not made toward the metrics which had been established as goals within six months, the company would be forced to find someone else to make it happen.

He agreed to accept the challenge, but what took place was a thorough disappointment. When the Lean change agent went on to his next assignment, the operations manager dismantled all the steps toward Lean Production. The Lean Production line was returned to its Fat way of working and to its old level of productivity. Shop floor workers became disheartened and cynical. Six months after the ultimatum, the plant was still only marginally profitable. The manager was given his walking papers, and a new manager was brought in.

Fortunately, many managers who start out strongly opposed to change end up as strong change agents themselves. When the general manager of a fairly efficient operation that had recently been acquired in a merger first saw his new management's presentation on Lean Production, his body language made it obvious he wasn't a happy camper. He sat in classic defensive posture—arms folded across his chest, a frown on his face. Now and then his eyes appeared to roll back.

This man saw the same presentation a second time when it was given to his new boss and the boss's immediate subordinates. The boss was unabashedly enthusiastic, and apparently his enthusiasm did not go unnoticed.

The general manager saw the presentation a third time when it was shown to key managers at his plant. By then, his demeanor had changed. The change agent received a warm welcome. Machines were moved and several batch processes eliminated. In no time, throughput picked up.

Workers received more authority. Teams brainstormed ways to do things better. New procedures supplanted old ones.

Brand Advertising

Soon the plant's productivity, including both direct and indirect labor, had improved by 40 percent. Output was way up with the same number of workers. Payroll was down significantly because outside, part-time help was no longer needed.

Then the inevitable backlash occurred. Middle managers who felt stripped of their authority clamored to have things returned to the old way. The general manager called his staff together. He explained that the organization was not turning back. That he was committed to Lean Transformation. That nothing would or could stop progress.

Difficulties surely would arise in the future, he added. They, too, would be met and overcome. Anyone holding out hope that the business would revert to the old way of working would be better off to let go of that illusion and get with the program. If they didn't like the new way, and weren't willing to help make it take hold, they should start looking for another job right now.

The crisis passed. The transformation continued. Today, that shop is a model Lean Enterprise.

Now, both of these managers were intelligent and had been successful in their careers. Both appeared to have had good reasons to want to make Lean Production work. Why did one refuse to accept the concept, while the other eventually embraced it as his own? Could the general manager have been more highly motivated than the operations manager? His plant had recently changed ownership as the result of a merger. He had new owners and new bosses who obviously were enthusiastic believers in Lean Production. The manager was in his fifties. Finding a new job at his age might not have been easy. Yet an ultimatum was neither issued nor ever needed.

The operations manager also was in his fifties. It was obvious that his superiors, too, believed enthusiastically in Lean Enterprise. He was actually told he would have to find a new job if he didn't make the transition happen. Yet it appears he didn't even try.

Why?

Might he have felt more secure because of his recent successes? He had indeed turned around a bad situation. He may have believed that the goals placed before him could be met using the old, traditional way of working. We suspect this was the case.

In contrast, the general manager saw Lean Production's potential. Again, we must ask, why?

Simply because some managers have a tendency to embrace Lean Enterprise while others just don't. It has nothing to do with education, experience or age. Potential Lean Managers will tend to describe themselves as "innovative," while potential concrete heads see themselves as "practical."

Potential Lean Managers are likely to focus on the future and the possibilities it holds. The possible is always out front, pulling on the imagination the way a magnet pulls on iron filings. The future holds more attraction than the past and present.

WORD AND IDEA PREFERENCES

CONCRETE HEADS	LEAN CHANGE AGENTS
• Past	• Future
• Experience	• Innovation
• Time-tested	• Speculative
• Traditional	• Imaginative
• Facts	• Hunches
• Sensible	• Possibilities
• No-nonsense	• Ingenuity
• Perspiration	• Inspiration
• Actual	• Intuitive
• Down-to-earth	• Theoretical

Potential concrete heads will describe themselves as being firmly grounded in reality. Like Detective Sergeant Joe Friday, they'll say they want facts. They remember facts. (They also believe in experience, and know from experience what works and what doesn't.) Potential foot draggers can never have enough facts. Once they've collected a pile, they'll want still more. Like Civil War General George McClellan with troops, horses and munitions, it may seem that they can never have enough facts to go into action.

Potential Lean Managers, on the other hand, don't make information gathering the end-all and be-all. Yes, they want and value data. But only enough of it to see a pattern, to support a hunch or theory, to justify making de Bono's intuitive leap to action based on the pattern or coherence that they see. For them, information simply "hangs together" to support a course of action. They may continue gathering data after they themselves are already convinced, but only to win over potential naysayers.

Lean Managers tolerate established procedures but willingly abandon any that can be shown to be counterproductive or irrelevant to the goals they seemingly serve.

Concrete heads, in contrast, are so in tune with established, time-honored institutions and procedures that they simply cannot understand anyone wanting to abandon or change them. Though visionary leadership isn't part of their makeup, they can, under normal circumstances, be effective administrators. In positions where the objective is to maintain status quo, they can even be valuable to an organization. But since Lean Transformation is neither normal circumstances nor devoted to maintaining the status quo, a different kind of Lean Manager is called for.

This kind of Lean Manager must be willing to step out front and take risks. He or she must be constantly on the lookout for new and better ways of doing things, stimulated by possibilities and constantly motivated by a restless feeling that there are better and more efficient ways.

Fat Agencies may have potential Lean Managers lurking within their organization charts, but the Fat Agency culture has made them experts at concealing this potential. Getting shot at whenever they raised their heads out of the foxhole has taught them to keep low profiles and keep their visions to themselves. (Look what visions did for Joan of Arc.) Only after some coaxing may they be willing to venture onto the battlefield again. Or only after some propaganda.

Remember our general manager? Only after seeing the same presentation on Lean Enterprise three times did he become a believer. That, plus

Brand Advertising

his superiors' very obvious enthusiasm, was enough to open his mind. He took the ball and ran with it.

No marketer worthy of the title should be the least bit surprised. As hundreds of thousands of dollars' worth of research has shown, repetition gets the message through. The first time someone sees something new, whether it's an ad or anything else, the usual reaction is to categorize it in terms of old knowledge. Suppose, for example, someone sees a purple cow. The reaction might be, "What's that? Oh, it's a cow, isn't it? Yes. Except, it's purple." Once they've got this in a pigeon hole, they feel free to move on.

The second time they see the cow, their reaction is likely to be more personally evaluative. "Aha, there's that purple cow again. Odd. But what does it mean to me?"

If they decide that the purple cow has relevance for them, the third and subsequent exposures will reinforce this. They may take action after the second exposure, or only after many more push them over the line. Our general manager, for example, got the point after the third exposure.

If, like the concrete head, someone decides that the purple cow has no relevance, no amount of repetition will change him. That person's mind is made up, so subsequent exposures go in one ear and out the other, accomplishing nothing.[20] So repetition can be important and helpful in making converts, but only if those potential converts are predisposed to innovation, only if they have a built-in uneasiness about the status quo, and only if they're future- and possibility-oriented.

Where propaganda doesn't work, a certain passage of time might.

It's naive to think that people who have been working a certain way all their life are going to embrace Lean Enterprise without a period of adjustment. They'll have to give up an approach they're accustomed to, an approach they've grown fond of and are comfortable with, an approach that's worked and taken them where they are. In some ways, it can be as traumatic as the death of a loved and very close relative.

It's not surprising, then, that when Lean Transformation threatens to doom everything line managers hold dear, they go through a process amazingly similar to the stages of grief that Dr. Elisabeth Kubler-Ross, the Swiss psychologist, identified among people dying of terminal illness: shock, denial, anger, bargaining, grieving and acceptance.

Brand Advertising

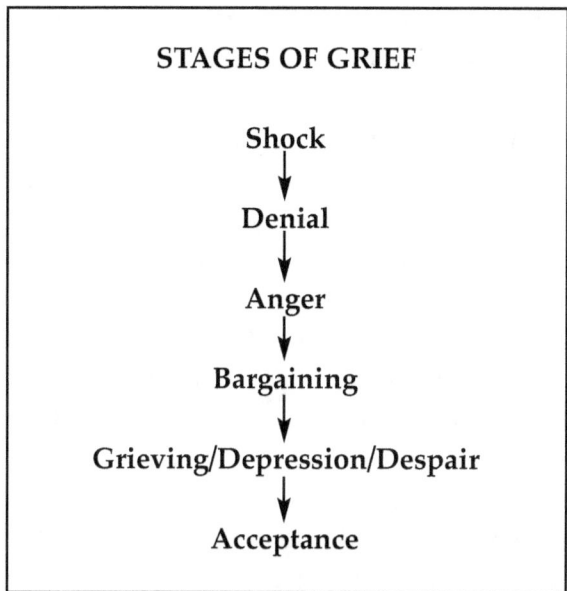

Stage One is shock, followed by denial, as in, "There's been a mistake. I'm sure I put a quarter in the parking meter." Yet the parking ticket's right there under the windshield wiper.

It happens all the time. When managers hear about the changes that switching to Lean Enterprise entails, they don't take them seriously. They believe that by ignoring Lean Transformation, it'll go away and life will go on as always. "This isn't happening," they may say. "If I just nod my head and smile, this will blow over."

If top management isn't totally committed, it will. But let's say they stick to their guns. The next stage will be anger. "The CEO can't mean it. Not after all I've accomplished. Well, this time I'm not going to do it. I'm valuable to this organization. I can't be forced to do this."

If top management continues to stick to its guns, the fourth stage—bargaining—follows. "Okay, I understand now. But some clients aren't going to like it. You'll have to agree, it's better not to rock the boat. This Broadband Creativity thing—showing clients all those sloppy roughs—they're not going to buy anything. We'll have to make some exceptions."

If top management once more holds its ground, the fifth stage is grief-like depression. Slumped shoulders. Dark circles under the eyes. It's as though the manager were saying, "I've tried to tell them, and they won't listen. There's only one thing left to do, and that's to go out into the parking lot and eat worms."

Once a line manager reaches this stage, Lean Transformation is practically home free. Because with a little moral support as needed, with a little more persuasion that it's a team effort and everyone is valuable, chances are he or she will move on to the sixth and last stage – acceptance. Then you've got yourself a Lean player.

Forewarned is forearmed. In briefings when Lean Transformation starts, managers and workers will need to hear that it's normal for them to pass through these stages, so that they'll understand what will happen to them. This won't circumvent the adjustment process, but it will help speed it along.

They'll also need to realize that to successfully transform the environment, to become a true Lean Agency, all the people in the organization will have to transform themselves as well.

Seeing themselves and others in a new light is the first step. It's something that they must do, not only in their jobs, but personally. Rather than thinking of themselves as associate creative directors or media planners, for example, they must see themselves as coaches or key players on a team. Rather than regarding others as co-workers or subordinates, they must come to view them as fellow team members.

How do you go about a personal transformation? How do you reprogram yourself? Some people will say they can't—"I was born this way. I can't be somebody I'm not." They're wrong. Anyone can change, whether by losing a hundred pounds or relating to others differently.

In *The Seven Habits of Highly Effective People*,[21] Stephen Covey writes about a realization that altered his life. He was wandering among stacks of books in a college library when he came across one that drew his interest. He opened it and was so moved by what he read that he reread the paragraph many times. It contained the simple idea that a gap exists between stimulus and response, and that the key to our growth and happiness is how we use it. We have the power to choose in that fraction of a second. If we see a photograph of a creamy chocolate sundae, we can choose to order and eat it, or we can decide on raspberry sherbet—or no dessert at all. If we see a fellow worker who happened to be our subordinate yesterday and who appears to be struggling with a particular task, we can order another worker who also happened to be our subordinate yesterday to help. Or we can be the one to help.

In *Don't Sweat the Small Stuff... and It's All Small Stuff*, Richard Carlson picks up on the same idea.[22] His advice is to always take a breath before speaking or taking action. If you adopt this, you'll rid yourself of the habit of reacting. You'll begin taking a considered approach, and taking a considered approach can lead to all sorts of good things such as better relationships with friends, family and co-workers. It can lead to a slimmer waistline. It can even lead to a successful transformation from commandant to coach.

Another way is to become what some have called a silent observer of yourself. The idea is to move your point of view outside your head and place it on your shoulder or the ceiling. Then watch yourself go about your business. You may see things that aren't helping you get where you want to go. From here, it's a short step to self-transformation. Especially if you take that breath before reacting.

But time—time for mourning or self-transformation—doesn't heal all wounds. There will still be some managers who simply can't make the transformation—not because they're unwilling to change, but because changing takes desire, and they don't have it.

Maybe their personal identities are too closely tied to their jobs. The jailer sees himself as a jailer; he can't picture himself as one of the inmates, even if he gets to be high scorer on the inmate basketball team. The commandant views himself as the commandant. Being commandant is what gives him his sense of self-worth. He simply will not allow himself to take the seeming demotion to coaching the cadets.

Which brings us to what top management must also bring to the Lean Transformation table—forethought. Agency leaders will have to decide in advance how they're going to handle the reluctant cases. How they'll stay alert to the stages and set a time limit for them to take place.

If a manager's not making progress, if it looks as though he or she will never be a team player, perhaps there's a solitary job that will still need doing in the new, Lean Agency. Or maybe something in media buying or accounting and billing. Move him or her into that job quickly. That way, a few bad apples won't be able to spoil the whole bunch.

Brand Advertising

For a Fat Agency to become a Lean Agency, not only must its line management be as strongly committed to change as its top management, but the managers themselves must have the imagination to focus on the future and the possibilities it holds, rather than on the past and its time-honored traditions. That's another reason why most will never make it.

Ironically, line management must simultaneously be two contradictory things: directive and empowering. Directive because strong, unambiguous leadership that's crystal-clear about the Lean Enterprise path is essential. Empowering because teams must have complete authority to achieve assigned results their own way.

As we noted earlier, it's not the workers who resist transformation. We've seen workers' attitudes change from glum to upbeat in just days—weeks at most. Even though they're accomplishing more, post-transformation surveys show they often believe they're not working as hard. Employee job satisfaction figures usually soar.

But as the workers welcome Lean Enterprise, the traditional organization will fight back. When an empowered team comes up with and implements ways to improve performance, they'll be charged up and ready to find more ways to improve, more *muda* to cut.

And that's when a backlash from the traditional organization will strike.

Why? Managers' turf has been threatened. Correctly or not, they see themselves losing control. A tug of war between early adapters and concrete heads will ensue. About 80% of the organization will be caught smack in the middle. The outcome will either be success or failure, and this will depend on how top management responds.

We're not all that optimistic about the response of Fat Agency leaders who've been working essentially the same way since fifteen to twenty years before some of their copywriters, art directors, media buyers and web designers were born. But if they really, truly want to become Lean Agencies, there are several things they can do.

The first is to be impatient. Especially when they hear things like, "You don't understand, this department is different." Or, "If we do that, it will disrupt the whole organization." They should be so impatient that anyone who says anything like that will get a very short time to either get on board or start pulling a resume together.

Brand Advertising

The second is to visibly side with the good guys. High-level leaders should work side-by-side with teams, joining them in identifying improvements they can make. Top managers should frequently visit offices or departments in the middle of transformation, to emphatically praise progress, or express impatience over the lack of it, to the team leader. They need to do some management by walking around, handing out positive strokes where progress and results are apparent and displaying displeasure where they aren't.

Third, they can be nosy. Senior management should regularly review progress reports and make it known that they're doing so. They should be on the lookout for positive trends, or the lack of them. If they don't see tangible progress within three to six months, something's wrong. More than likely, the wrong team, or individual, is leading the charge. It's time to reevaluate.

Fourth, they can be time-conscious. Moving too slowly in transforming to a Lean Agency dissipates valuable momentum and enthusiasm. Moving too quickly can overwhelm the infrastructure, creating glitches, igniting sparks of discontent and giving naysayers gasoline to pour on them.

Finally, they can be communicative. It's ironic that nobody screws up internal communications like people in the business of communicating. So Fat Agency leaders should treat the Lean Agency transformation as a valued client, its workforce as the target audience, and use every tool at their disposal, from printed and e-mail newsletters to strategy documents, special web sites and chat rooms and instant messaging, as the media schedule. Nothing makes something so real or so urgent as putting it in writing.

The actual target audience will be 80 percent of the Fat Agency workforce. Like most things in life, workforces follow a bell curve. About 10 percent of the workers and managers will start working like a Lean Agency so fast, it won't even seem like a transition. Another 10 percent, the concrete heads, never will. The 80 percent in the middle are up for grabs, and they'll need live, in-person communication.

So when the time comes for transformation to start, management will need to get people together and let them know what's going to happen and what they can expect. A meeting or series of meetings should communicate plans, objectives, strategies, and the reasons for the transformation. The purpose of the meetings is to create a shared vision for the immediate future, a road map that eliminates as much uncertainty as possible during what's sure to be an uncertain time in the agency.

People will need to understand why the decision to go Lean has been made, why it's essential to staying competitive, why it's the only sure way to achieve the company's goals. And they'll need to know how the transformation will affect them—that their value as workers will be enhanced, that the cross- training that they get will make them multi-skilled, that as they become more and more empowered in a better, team-empowered working environment, they'll become more and more satisfied with their jobs, that the company will grow and expand, creating more opportunities which may flow to them.

Tempting as it might sound, top management won't be able to whip the hard-care reactionaries into line. But maybe the powerful psychological motivation of a shared goal will accomplish what twenty lashes can't. The need to keep the corporate ship afloat can go a long way toward putting down the mutineers.

A shared objective can be a powerful rallying point. It can make individuals buy into something bigger than themselves. We often refer to this as the big goal. For a football team it might be the Super Bowl. In tennis, the Davis Cup. In soccer, the World Cup. In advertising, it could be an X-percent jump in new business, or selling Y-percent of new campaigns the first time out, or winning a particular pitch, or growing to number-two agency in the market, or winning a Clio, Effie or One Show pencil, whatever—so long as it requires Lean Enterprise to reach it.

Like the prospect of being hanged in the morning, nothing concentrates the mind like the pressing need to achieve a big goal within a relatively short time. When John F. Kennedy announced the big goal of putting a man on the Moon by 1970, it pulled the nation together and won the space race (as well as giving too many politicians the opportunity to say, "If we can put a man on the Moon, why can't we [politician's pet pork project goes here]").

This is what Fat Agency leaders striving for Leanness want their agency's people to do—pull together and win.

Maybe the goal is creating a new advantage over the competition.

Going Lean should open up the possibilities, particularly if Broadband Creativity explores and defines them. The key will be to determine which is most significant in the minds of both managers and clients. One advantage may be that with multifunctional teams practicing Broadband Creativity, the agency will be able to create effective campaigns faster. Maybe increased productivity and decreased *muda* will let the agency undercut competitors' pricing.

After discovering as many compelling practical advantages as it can, top management should list them. In writing, but not in any order of priority. Showing or presenting the list to line managers (and maybe to empowered teams), and asking their help in deciding which core value the agency should hang its hat on once the transformation to Leanness is made, will accomplish several things.

It will call attention to the strategic advantages the agency will enjoy and bring managers together in an effort to decide how best to capitalize on them.

If all goes well, the effort to put a finger on the most important value may be just the mechanism to rally doubters and dissenters in a way that makes transformation easier. People feel good when their help and opinions are sought, but this is not just a feel-good exercise. They may come up with more, and better, ideas than top management did. But regardless of what they come up with, they'll feel a closer bond to the company.

After all, they're defining their own core value. The one they offer customers above all else. The one they offer most convincingly, because they own it. The one they'll put their full efforts behind to accomplish, through Lean Transformation.

That can go a long way towards making everyone in the Fat Agency *want* to be part of its transformation into a Lean Agency. But wanting isn't enough. Transformations depend on doing, and there are two main approaches to getting everyone to start doing.

One is called the "define and convince" approach. Here, someone assigned as the change leader (or maybe several people assigned as the change team) defines the agency's specific recipe for change and convinces everyone else to follow it. This approach works best in small agencies where everyone knows and more or less trusts and respects each other.

The other is called the "participative" approach, because here everyone's a cook creating the recipe. The agency leader defines the goals and challenges the workforce to make the changes necessary to achieve them. There will be large group meetings for convergence and decision-making and smaller group work sessions for coming up with new ideas and trying them out.

But once the leaders have laid the groundwork, they need to step back and trust the workers to do the work. With this approach, there are no change leaders forcing compliance, because everyone, at all levels, from all functional areas, works together. Within teams, leaders will set targets and make strategic decisions, while members will work out the best tactics for hitting those targets. The only things that come down from the top are definition (of Lean Enterprise) and basic background information.

Regardless of approach, it makes sense to begin the transformation in the area closest to the customer. In manufacturing, this is final assembly. In advertising, it's campaign development. It also makes sense to begin with the personnel who work in this area, in this case one or more empowered, multifunctional teams.

And though command-and-control metrics (like the old Soviet five-year-plan production quotas) are anathema to a Lean Agency, there should be some measurements. Measurements having to do with how long it takes to produce work, inside and outside costs, how well client sales or awareness goals are being met, and the like.

Again, the purpose here is not to check up on people, but to gauge progress and, once the transformation's complete, to maintain gains.

But a true Lean Transformation is never complete. Because once the agency is truly Lean, its way of doing things becomes its new baseline—to be examined, explored, *kaizen*ed, improved, transformed, evaluated and examined all over again.

It takes a lot of work and even more commitment for a Fat Agency to transform itself into a Lean Agency. And even though the gains far outweigh the effort, we don't think many will even try.

It took more than two decades—decades of cheap offshore labor, Japanese quality and price competition, and computerized automation—to get American manufacturers to evolve from batch processing and inventory control to just-in-time, continuous-flow Lean Production. And many manufacturers, particularly in and around Detroit, still haven't.

You'd think that advertising agencies, with far less in the way of capital-intensive heavy machinery and apparent commitment to innovation, wouldn't still be following a half-century-old structure. But for all the talk of innovation and imagination, of breakthrough work and thinking outside the box, Fat Agencies—and that means just about all advertising agencies—are better at talking the talk than walking the walk. If you don't believe this, leaf through any magazine, or spend an hour or two watching television, or actually look at the popup and banner ads you usually try to ignore on your computer screen, and see how much innovation and imagination there is in the ads and commercials that are their products.

The truth is, Lean Enterprise goes against the grain of just about everything that Fat Agencies have held dear since the first pyramid-shaped organizational chart was drawn. And, short of massive losses of business to a new, Lean Agency competitor, it's hard for outside forces to change that.

If you're a marketer who wants to put Lean Advertising to work to create brand advertising that makes an emotional connection with prospective customers, you can do one of two things.

The first is to demand that your Fat Agency set up a Lean Mini-Agency—a dedicated, empowered, multifunctional team for your brand's work. If your account represents a big enough part of their revenue, the threat of your leaving if this isn't done should constitute a big enough sense of crisis to get their attention and get them off the dime.

But that's a far from ideal solution. An advertising agency can't really work half Fat and half Lean. Trying to be both creates corporate schizophrenia in the agency by sending out mixed messages about what its culture and operational philosophy really are. At best, it sends out the message that the agency leadership's commitment to Leanness is something less than total.

Moreover, when Fat and Lean operations work side by side, it's usually the Lean operation that's the loser. Not because Lean isn't superior—it is, head and shoulders—but because the Fat operation it's coexisting with gives the agency people tons of excuses for foot-dragging. It can encourage naysayers to go through the motions, doubters to wait and see and uncommitted managers and workers to just stand around and kick the tires instead of strapping in and driving.

So when you come right down to it, being committed to becoming a Lean Agency is like being pregnant—either you are or you aren't.

So if you're not a big enough client to demand that your Fat Agency change through and through, you have only one other alternative.

And that's to go out and find a small, creative advertising agency and marketing communications firm that was built as a Lean Agency from the beginning.

End Notes

Preface
1. Search Engine Optimization [SEO] involves creating written and other content with the goal of attracting web users searching specific key words and phrases.

Chapter 1
1 http://www.nytimes.com/2012/03/25/books/review/the-righteous-mind-by-jonathan-haidt.html?_r=1&pagewanted=all
2 http://adage.com/article/news/coke-olympics-link-healthful-lifestyles/235747/
3 http://adage.com/article/cmo-strategy/questions-mcdonald-s-kevin-newell/235649/
4 http://adage.com/article/global-news/expect-major-marketers-olympic-pushes/235872/
5 http://www.mediapost.com/publications/article/180382/mcdonalds-olympic-ads-fuel-backlash-on-twitter.html?edition=49814#axzz2fkz1lpBK

Chapter 2
1 http://adage.com/article/cmo-strategy/pepsi-burger-king-news-signal-end-social-media/149523/
2 http://www.telegraph.co.uk/technology/social-media/8912701/Companies-must-learn-from-Qantas-Twitter-gaffe-and-TripAdvisor-blackmails.html

Chapter 3
2. Larry Dobrow, *When Advertising Tried Harder,* New York: Friendly Press, Inc., 1984
3. Ibid.
4. Ibid.
5. James C. Collins and Jerry I. Porras, *Built to Last,* New York: HarperBusiness paperback edition, 1992
6. Ibid.
7. Ibid.
8. Ibid.

End Notes Continued

Chapter 7

19. Mitchell Ginsburg, "Comprehending Kahneman," *The Jerusalem Report,* February 10, 2003
20. From 1979 through 1986, while at The Martin Agency, Steve Martin studied the effects of frequency. He wrote a number of articles on this subject that appeared in the trade publication, *Marketing & Media Decisions.*
21. Stephen R. Covey, *The Seven Habits of Highly Effective People,* New York: Simon & Schuster, 1989.
22. Richard Carlson, PH.D, *Don't Sweat the Small Stuff . . . and It's all small Stuff,* New York: Hyperion, 1997.

www.ingramcontent.com/pod-product-compliance
Lightning Source LLC
Chambersburg PA
CBHW070253190526
45169CB00001B/395